# THE
# LIFE OF
# CHRIST

*By* Charles L. Allen

# CHARLES L. ALLEN

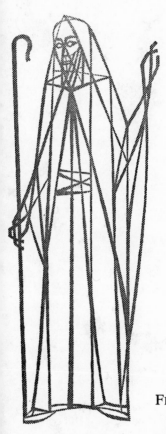

# THE
# LIFE of
# CHRIST

FLEMING H. REVELL COMPANY
OLD TAPPAN, NEW JERSEY

To
*the members of*
THE FIRST METHODIST CHURCH
HOUSTON, TEXAS
*whose love and prayers make my work as
their pastor a most happy experience*

# The Four Gospels in One

I have said to many people, "Read one of the four Gospels ten times. Read it thoughtfully and prayerfully each time, and it will have a deep and abiding influence upon your life." Many have reported thrilling results of such a reading.

Jesus Christ is so wonderful that even from the cold type of the printed page His power is felt by one who reads. We read in the book of Acts, "Now when they saw the boldness of Peter and John, and perceived that they were unlearned and ignorant men, they marveled; and they took knowledge of them, that they had been with Jesus." No one can have fellowship with Christ without being noticeably blessed. In the repeated reading of one of the Gospels that fellowship with Him becomes more real and complete.

In my own readings, I find that any of the Gospels—Matthew, Mark, Luke or John—bless me equally, as far as I can tell. Each tells the same story. Yet as I read one of the Gospels, I realize that I am missing certain things which one or more of the other Gospel writers included. Actually it takes all four of the Gospels to complete the story. Thus the preparation of this book.

This *Life of Christ* is not one which I have written. Rather have I carefully compared the four Gospels and arranged them into one story.

There are many books which one may use to aid in a study of the Gospels, verse by verse. The aim of this book is to give the panoramic picture through the eyes of those who remembered Christ in the days of His flesh. I have sought neither to add to nor to take away from their story.

I have left Jesus' words in the language of the King James Version. Though I appreciate the many scholarly translations which we now have, still I find greatest inspiration in the lofty language of the version which I first read and came to love.

Many books have been written about Jesus Christ. On the shelves of my study are a hundred and more of those books which have enlarged my understanding of the Lord. Yet I find some authors have used their imaginations too freely. Some seem to have taken away or added to the story almost at will. Also, I have found this to be true about the motion pictures which tell about Jesus' life.

The four Gospels were written simply, without exaggerations and dramatic fancies of the authors. I believe them to have been truly inspired by God. In them we are told all that is necessary for a saving knowledge of Jesus Christ.

The aim of this book is to present Matthew, Mark, Luke and John in one continuous story. In reading this story, one cannot but be blessed by it.

Mrs. Marion Hutchinson, my secretary for many years, has been my partner in this endeavor. She gave me valuable counsel, and carefully prepared the manuscript. In addition, her assuming of many other duties of mine enabled me to give the many hours necessary for this work. I appreciate her very much.

Charles L. Allen

# Contents

# THE
# LIFE OF
# CHRIST

# THE YEARS
# OF PREPARATION

## ✠ *The First Thirty Years*

The birth of Jesus happened in this way. *The Annunci-*
When his mother Mary was engaged to be married to *ation*
Joseph, before they came together, it was found that she
was with child—of the Holy Ghost. An angel came to
her and said, "Hail, thou that art highly favoured! The
Lord is with thee, blessed art thou among women." But
she was disturbed by what the angel said and did not
understand.

And the angel said to her, "Fear not, Mary: for thou
hast found favour with God. And, behold, thou shalt
conceive in thy womb, and bring forth a son, and shalt
call his name JESUS. He shall be great, and shall be called
the Son of the Highest: and the Lord God shall give unto
him the throne of his father David: and he shall reign
over the house of Jacob for ever; and of his kingdom
there shall be no end."

Then Mary said to the angel, "How shall this be, seeing
I know not a man?" And the angel replied, "The Holy
Ghost shall come upon thee, and the power of the Highest shall overshadow thee: therefore also that holy thing
which shall be born of thee shall be called the Son of
God. And, behold, thy cousin Elisabeth, she hath also
conceived a son in her old age: and this is the sixth month

with her, who was called barren. For with God nothing shall be impossible."

Mary then said, "Behold the handmaid of the Lord; be it unto me according to thy word." And the angel departed from her.

Then her husband, Joseph, being a fair man, and not willing to publicly embarrass her, had in mind to hide her away. But while he thought about it, an angel appeared to him in a dream, and said, "Joseph, thou son of David, fear not to take unto thee Mary thy wife: for that which is conceived in her is of the Holy Ghost. And she shall bring forth a son, and thou shalt call his name JESUS: for he shall save his people from their sins."

When Joseph woke up, he did as the angel told him, and married Mary, but would have no relations with her before her son was born.

*Mary's Visit to Elisabeth*

Before long Mary went to the city of Judah to see Elisabeth. When Elisabeth heard Mary's hello, her own baby leaped within her. She felt the Spirit of God and with a loud voice said, "Blessed art thou among women, and blessed is the fruit of thy womb. And whence is this to me, that the mother of my Lord should come to me? For, lo, as soon as the voice of thy salutation sounded in mine ears, the babe leaped in my womb for joy. And blessed is she that believed: for there shall be a performance of these things which were told her from the Lord."

Mary then said:

"My soul doth magnify the Lord,
And my spirit hath rejoiced in God my Saviour.
For he hath regarded the low estate of his handmaiden:
For, behold, from henceforth all generation shall call me blessed.
For he that is mighty hath done to me great things;
And holy is his name.
And his mercy is on them that fear him

14 |

From generation to generation.
He hath shewed strength with his arm;
He hath scattered the proud in the imagination of
　　their hearts.
He hath put down the mighty from their seats,
And exalted them of low degree.
He hath filled the hungry with good things;
And the rich he hath sent empty away,
He hath holpen his servant Israel,
In remembrance of his mercy,
As he spake to our fathers,
To Abraham, and to his seed for ever."

And Mary stayed with her about three months, and
returned home.

　　　　　　When the time came, Elisabeth gave birth to *The Birth of*
a son and her neighbors and kinfolk heard how God had *John the*
blessed her and they rejoiced with her. *Baptist*

On the eighth day when they came to circumcise the
child, they were going to name the child Zacharias, after
his father. His mother spoke up and said, "Not so; but he
shall be called John." They reminded her that no one
in her family had ever been named John. Zacharias was
deaf and dumb but they made signs to him. He asked for
something to write on and wrote, "His name is John."
Immediately he was able to talk. He praised God and
told about how John would be a prophet of God.

The baby grew and became spiritually strong. He
lived out away from people until it was time for him
to appear publicly in Israel.

　　　　　　At this time Caesar Augustus sent out a decree *The Birth of*
that everyone should be registered. This happened when *Jesus*
Cyrenius was governor of Syria. Everyone went to his
own city to register. Because Joseph was a descendent of
David, he went to Bethlehem in Judea to register, together with his wife, Mary, who was expecting a child.

While they were there it came time for her baby to be
born, and she gave birth to her first son. She wrapped　　| 15

him up and laid him in a manger, because there was not room for them in the inn.

*The Angel's Appearance to Shepherds*

Nearby there were shepherds out in the field watching over their sheep during the night. An angel appeared before them, the light of God began to shine all around them, and they were much afraid. The angel said to them, "Fear not: for, behold, I bring you good tidings of great joy, which shall be to all people. For unto you is born this day in the city of David a Saviour, which is Christ the Lord. And this shall be a sign unto you; Ye shall find the babe wrapped in swaddling clothes, lying in a manger." At that moment a heavenly choir appeared singing:

"Glory to God in the highest,
And on earth peace, good will toward men."

After the angels had gone, the shepherds said to each other, "Let us now go even unto Bethlehem, and see this thing which is come to pass, which the Lord hath made known unto us."

They hurried and found Mary, and Joseph, and the baby lying in a manger. When they had seen it, they told all around what had been told them about this child. The people who heard it were amazed at what the shepherds said. But Mary made mental note of everything and thought about it carefully. The shepherds returned filled with praise to God for what they had heard and seen.

*The Circumcision*

At the end of eight days it was time for the circumcising of the child. He was named Jesus, which was the name given him by the angel in the very beginning.

*The Wise Men*

At the time that Jesus was born, when Herod was king, wise men came from the East, asking, "Where is he that is born King of the Jews? for we have seen his star in the east, and are come to worship him."

When Herod heard this, it worried him, as it did all the people in Jerusalem. He called in all the chief priests and scribes and demanded them to tell him where Christ

was born. They replied, "In Bethlehem of Judea: for it is
written by the prophet,

> And thou Bethlehem, in the land of Juda,
> Art not the least among the princes of Juda:
> For out of thee shall come a Governor,
> That shall rule my people Israel."

Then Herod, when he had privately called the wise
men, questioned them thoroughly as to what time the
star appeared. He sent them to Bethlehem and said, "Go
and search diligently for the young child; and when ye
have found him, bring me word again, that I may come
and worship him also." When they had heard what the
king had to say, they left; and the star which they had
seen in the East went before them, until it came and stood
over the place where the young child was. When they
saw the star it brought great joy to them.

When they came into the house, they saw the young
child with Mary his mother, and they knelt down and
worshiped him. When they opened their treasures, they
presented to him gifts of gold and frankincense and
myrrh. Because they were warned by God in a dream
that they should not return to Herod, they went back
home by another road.

After the wise men had gone, an angel appeared to Joseph in a dream and said, "Arise, and take
the young child and his mother, and flee into Egypt; and
be thou there until I bring thee word: for Herod will
seek the young child to destroy him." That night Joseph
left for Egypt and stayed there until Herod died. Thus it
was fulfilled what the prophet had said, "Out of Egypt
have I called my son."

When Herod saw that he had been tricked by the wise
men, he was very angry and had all the children killed
who were in and around Bethlehem and who were two
years old and under. Thus were fulfilled the words of
the prophet Jeremiah:

*The Flight
Into Egypt,
Herod's Mas-
sacre, Return
to Nazareth*

| 17

"In Rama was there a voice heard,
Lamentation, and weeping, and great mourning,
Rachel weeping for her children,
And would not be comforted, because they are not."

After Herod died, an angel of the Lord appeared in a
dream to Joseph in Egypt and said, "Arise, and take the
young child and his mother, and go into the land of
Israel: for they are dead which sought the young child's
life." And he went toward Israel. But when he heard that
Archelaus reigned in Judea in the place of his father
Herod, he was afraid to go further, so he turned into a
part of Galilee and lived in the town of Nazareth.

*The Presenta-
tion in the
Temple*

Later they carried Jesus to Jerusalem to be
dedicated to God in the temple, and to offer the sacrifice
of a pair of turtledoves or two young pigeons, which was
according to the law.

In Jerusalem there was a man whose name was Simeon.
He was a very good and righteous man, who had been
promised by God that he would see the Christ before he
died. When the parents brought Jesus in, Simeon held
the baby in his arms, and he said to God,

"Lord, now lettest thou thy servant depart in peace,
According to thy word:
For mine eyes have seen thy salvation,
Which thou hast prepared before the face of all people;
A light to lighten the Gentiles,
And the glory of thy people Israel."

There was a prophetess, Anna, who was very old and
had been a widow for eighty-four years, after having
been married for seven years. She spent all her time praising God in the temple. She saw the child, thanked God
for him and talked of him to all those in Jerusalem who
looked forward to being saved by God.

*The Boy Jesus
in the Temple*

18 |

Every year Jesus' parents went to Jerusalem
for the feast of the Passover. The year Jesus was twelve
they went as usual, along with many other people. After-

ward, they started back home but Jesus lingered behind
in Jerusalem. Joseph and Mary supposed he was in the
group until that night when they could not find him.

They went back to Jerusalem and after searching for
three days found him in the temple. He was with the
teachers, listening to their conversations and asking them
questions. These men were surprised at how much he
understood and the answers he gave. When Joseph and
Mary saw Jesus, they could hardly believe it, and Mary
said, "Son, why hast thou thus dealt with us? behold, thy
father and I have sought thee sorrowing."

Jesus replied, "How is it that ye sought me? wist ye not
that I must be about my Father's business?" But his
parents did not understand. He then went back home
with them and was an obedient son; but his mother wondered about the meaning of many of the things he said.

And Jesus grew in mind and body and in his relations
with God and men.

# THE YEAR
# OF BEGINNING

✠ *The First Year of Christ's Ministry*

*The Ministry
of John the
Baptist*

During the fifteenth year of the reign of Tiberius Caesar, Pontius Pilate was Governor of Judea, Herod was prince of Galilee, his brother Philip was prince of Ituraea and Trachonitis, Lysanias was prince of Abilene, and Annas and Caiaphas were the high priests.

At this time the word of God came to John, the son of Zacharias, who was out in the wilderness. He came into the area of Jordan, saying, "Repent ye: for the kingdom of heaven is at hand." John was the one who had been spoken of by the prophet Isaiah:

"Behold, I send my messenger before thy face,
Which shall prepare thy way before thee;
The voice of one crying in the wilderness,
Prepare ye the way of the Lord,
Make his paths straight.
Every valley shall be filled
And every mountain and hill shall be brought low;
And the crooked shall be made straight,
And the rough ways shall be made smooth;
And all flesh shall see the salvation of God."

Large crowds came to hear John preach, they confessed their sins and were baptized by him in the Jordan river.

John wore a camel's hair coat and a skirt made out of skin. He ate locusts and wild honey.

When he saw so many of the Pharisees and Sadducees come to hear him, he said to them, "O generation of vipers, who hath warned you to flee from the wrath to come? Bring forth therefore fruits meet for repentance: and think not to say within yourselves, We have Abraham to our father: for I say unto you, that God is able of these stones to raise up children unto Abraham. And now also the ax is laid unto the root of the trees; therefore every tree which bringeth not forth good fruit is hewn down, and cast into the fire."

The people asked him, "What shall we do?"

He answered them, "He that hath two coats, let him impart to him that hath none; and he that hath meat, let him do likewise."

Also, tax collectors came to him to be baptized and they asked him, "Master, what shall we do?" He replied, "Exact no more than that which is appointed you."

Likewise the soldiers asked him, "What shall we do?" He said to them, "Do violence to no man, neither accuse any falsely; and be content with your wages."

As the people were expecting great things from John, and wondering if he were Christ, he said to them, "I indeed baptize you with water; but one mightier than I cometh, the latchet of whose shoes I am not worthy to unloose: he shall baptize you with the Holy Ghost and with fire: whose fan is in his hand, and he will thoroughly purge his floor, and will gather the wheat into his garner; but the chaff he will burn with fire unquenchable." And he said many other things to them.

Jesus came from Galilee to John at the Jordan to be baptized. John discouraged him, saying, "I have need to be baptized of thee, and comest thou to me?" *The Baptism of Jesus*

Jesus replied, "Suffer it to be so now, for thus it becometh us to fulfil all righteousness."

Then John baptized him and, when Jesus came out of

the water, the heavens opened up and he saw the Spirit of God coming down like a dove and lighting upon him. Then a voice from heaven said, "This is my beloved Son, in whom I am well pleased."

At this time Jesus was about thirty years of age.

*The Tempta-*
*tion of Jesus*

Afterward Jesus felt led by the Spirit to get away into the wilderness. There he was tempted by the devil. He went without food for forty days and nights and he became very hungry. Then the tempter came to him and said, "If thou be the Son of God, command that these stones be made bread." Jesus answered him, "It is written, Man shall not live by bread alone, but by every word that proceedeth out of the mouth of God."

Then the devil took him up on a high mountain and showed him all the kingdoms of the world in a moment of time. The devil said to him, "All this power will I give thee, and the glory of them: for that is delivered unto me; and to whomsoever I will I give it. If thou therefore wilt worship me, all shall be thine."

Jesus replied, "Get thee behind me, Satan: for it is written, Thou shalt worship the Lord thy God, and him only shalt thou serve."

Then the devil brought Jesus to Jerusalem, set him on a pinnacle of the temple and said to him, "If thou be the Son of God, cast thyself down from hence: for it is written, He shall give his angels charge over thee, to keep thee: and in their hands they shall bear thee up, lest at any time thou dash thy foot against a stone."

Jesus answered, "It is said, Thou shalt not tempt the Lord thy God."

When the devil ended these temptations, he left him for the time being. Then angels came and ministered unto him. Jesus returned to Galilee in the power of the Spirit and news about him went throughout the countryside. He taught in their synagogues and was praised by all.

*The Witness*
*of John*
22 |

The Jews sent priests and Levites from Jerusalem to ask John, "Who art thou?" He told them, "I am not the Christ."

They asked, "What then? Art thou Elias?" He said, "I am not." "Art thou that prophet?" He answered, "No." Then they asked, "Who art thou? that we may give an answer to them that sent us. What sayest thou of thyself?" He said, "I am the voice of one crying in the wilderness, Make straight the way of the Lord, as said the prophet Esaias."

These men who had come to talk to John then inquired, "Why baptizest thou then, if thou be not that Christ, nor Elias, neither that prophet?" John replied to them, "I baptize with water: but there standeth one among you, whom ye know not; he it is, who coming after me is preferred before me, whose shoe's latchet I am not worthy to unloose."

This happened in Bethabara beyond Jordan, where John was baptizing.

The next day John saw Jesus coming toward *The Lamb of* him and he said, "Behold the Lamb of God, which taketh *God* away the sin of the world. This is he of whom I said, After me cometh a man which is preferred before me: for he was before me. And I knew him not: but that he should be made manifest to Israel, therefore am I come baptizing with water." Then John testified, "I saw the Spirit descending from heaven like a dove, and it abode upon him. And I knew him not: but he that sent me to baptize with water, the same said unto me, Upon whom thou shalt see the Spirit descending and remaining on him, the same is he which baptizeth with the Holy Ghost. And I saw, and bare record that this is the Son of God."

The day after, John, while standing with two of his disciples, saw Jesus walking along and he said, "Behold the Lamb of God." The two disciples heard his remark and followed Jesus. Jesus turned and saw them following and said to them, "What seek ye?" They replied, "Master, where dwellest thou?" He said to them, "Come and see." They came where he was stopping and stayed with him that night, for it was then about four o'clock in the afternoon.

*Andrew
Brings Simon
to Jesus*

One of the two which heard John and followed Jesus was Andrew, Simon Peter's brother. The first thing he did after leaving Jesus was to find his brother Simon and say to him, "We have found the Messiah," and he brought him to Jesus. When Jesus saw him, he said, "Thou art Simon, the son of John; thou shalt be called Cephas" (which means a stone).

*Philip Brings
Nathanael to
Jesus*

The next day Jesus decided to go to Galilee. He found Philip and said to him, "Follow me." Philip was from Bethsaida, the home of Andrew and Peter. Philip found Nathanael and said to him, "We have found him, of whom Moses, in the law, and the prophets did write, Jesus of Nazareth, the son of Joseph." Nathanael said to him, "Can there any good thing come out of Nazareth?" Philip said to him, "Come and see."

Jesus saw Nathanael coming to him and said of him, "Behold, an Israelite indeed, in whom is no guile!" Nathanael said to him, "Whence knowest thou me?" Jesus replied, "Before that Philip called thee, when thou wast under a fig tree, I saw thee." Nathanael answered, "Rabbi, thou art the Son of God; thou art the King of Israel." Jesus said, "Because I said unto thee, I saw thee under the fig tree, believest thou? Thou shalt see greater things than these." And he said to him, "Verily, verily, I say unto you, hereafter ye shall see heaven open, and the angels of God ascending and descending upon the Son of Man."

*The First
Miracle*

Two days later there was a marriage in Cana in Galilee. The mother of Jesus was there. Jesus and his disciples were invited, also.

When they wanted wine, the mother of Jesus said to him, "They have no wine." Jesus said to her, "Woman, what have I to do with thee? Mine hour is not yet come." His mother said to the servants, "Whatsoever he saith unto you, do it."

There were six water-pots of stone sitting nearby, as was the Jewish custom, each one holding twenty to thirty gallons. Jesus said to them, "Fill the waterpots with water." And they filled them up to the brim. Then he said to them, "Draw out now, and bear unto the governor of the feast," and they did so. When the ruler of the feast had tasted the water that had been changed into wine, and knew not where it came from (but the servants knew), he called the bridegroom and said to him, "Every man at the beginning doth set forth good wine; and when men have well drunk, then that which is worse: but thou hast kept the good wine until now."

This was the first of the miracles of Jesus through which he manifested his glory, and it led his disciples to believe on him.

After this he went down to Capernaum with his mother, brothers, and his disciples but they did not stay there many days. As it was time for the Feast of the Passover, he went to Jerusalem. There many believed in him when they saw the miracles he did. But Jesus did not trust himself to them. He so thoroughly understood men that he did not need others to tell him what men are like.

There was a Pharisee by the name of Nico- *Nicodemus* demus, who was a ruler of the Jews. He came to Jesus one night and said to him, "Rabbi, we know that thou art a teacher come from God: for no man can do these miracles that thou doest, except God be with him." Jesus replied, "Verily, verily, I say unto thee, except a man be born again, he cannot see the kingdom of God." Nicodemus said to him, "How can a man be born when he is old? Can he enter the second time into his mother's womb and be born?" Jesus answered, "Verily, verily, I say unto thee, Except a man be born of water, and of the Spirit, he cannot enter into the kingdom of God. That which is born of the flesh is flesh, and that which is born of the Spirit is spirit. Marvel not that I said unto thee, ye must be born again. The wind bloweth where it listeth, and thou hearest the sound thereof, but canst not tell whence it cometh, and whither it goeth: so is every one that is born of the Spirit."

Nicodemus said, "How can these things be?" Jesus

| 25

replied, "Art thou a master of Israel, and knowest not these things? Verily, verily, I say unto thee, we speak that we do know, and testify that we have seen; and ye receive not our witness. If I have told you earthly things, and ye believe not, how shall ye believe if I tell you of heavenly things? And no man hath ascended up to heaven, but he that came down from heaven, even the Son of man which is in heaven. And as Moses lifted up the serpent in the wilderness, even so must the Son of man be lifted up: that whosoever believeth in him should not perish, but have eternal life. For God so loved the world, that he gave his only begotten Son, that whosoever believeth in him should not perish, but have everlasting life. For God sent not his Son into the world to condemn the world; but that the world through him might be saved. He that believeth on him is not condemned: but he that believeth not is condemned already, because he hath not believed in the name of the only begotten Son of God. And this is the condemnation, that light is come into the world, and men loved darkness rather than light, because their deeds were evil. For every one that doeth evil hateth the light, neither cometh to the light, lest his deeds should be reproved. But he that doeth truth cometh to the light, that his deeds may be made manifest, that they are wrought in God."

*Christ's Ju-*
*dean Ministry* After this Jesus and his disciples went into the land of Judea where they stayed for a while and baptized.

Also John was baptizing in Aenon, near Salim, because water there was plentiful. Then there came up a question between some of John's disciples and the Jews about purification and they said to John, "Rabbi, he that was with thee beyond Jordan, to whom thou barest witness, behold, the same baptizeth, and all men come to him."

John replied, "A man can receive nothing, except it be given him from heaven. Ye yourselves bear me witness, that I said, I am not the Christ, but that I am sent before him. He that hath the bride is the bridegroom: but the friend of the bridegroom, which standeth and heareth him, rejoiceth greatly because of the bridegroom's voice: this my joy therefore is fulfilled. He must increase, but I must decrease. He that cometh from above is above all: he that is of the earth is earthly, and speaketh of the earth: he that cometh from heaven is above all. And what he hath seen and heard, that he testifieth; and no man receiveth his testimony. He that hath received his testimony hath set to his seal that God is true. For he whom God hath sent speaketh the words of God: for God giveth not the Spirit by measure unto him. The Father loveth the Son, and hath given all things into his hand. He that believeth on the Son hath everlasting life: but he that believeth not the Son shall not see life; but the wrath of God abideth on him."

When Jesus learned that the report had reached the Pharisees that he made and baptized more disciples than John, though Jesus himself did not baptize but his disciples did, he left Judea and again went to Galilee.

It was necessary for him to go through Samaria. He came to the city of Samaria which is called Sychar, near the place that Jacob gave to his son Joseph. Jacob's well was there. It was about noon and, being weary because of his travel, he sat down by the well.

A Samaritan woman came to draw some *The Woman* water. Jesus said to her, "Give me to drink," for his dis- *of Samaria* ciples had gone into the city to buy food. The woman said to him, "How is it that thou, being a Jew, askest drink of me, which am a woman of Samaria?" (for the Jews had nothing to do with the Samaritans).

Jesus replied to her, "If thou knewest the gift of God, and who it is that saith to thee, Give me to drink; thou wouldest have asked of him, and he would have given thee living water."

The woman said to him, "Sir, thou hast nothing to draw with, and the well is deep: from whence then hast thou that living water? Art thou greater than our father

Jacob, which gave us the well, and drank thereof himself, and his children, and his cattle?" Jesus replied, "Whosoever drinketh of this water shall thirst again: but whosoever drinketh of the water that I shall give him shall
never thirst; but the water that I shall give him shall be
in him a well of water springing up into everlasting life."

The woman said, "Sir, give me this water, that I thirst
not, neither come hither to draw." Jesus told her, "Go,
call thy husband, and come hither." The woman answered, "I have no husband." Jesus said to her, "Thou
hast well said, I have no husband: for thou hast had five
husbands; and he whom thou now hast is not thy husband: in that saidst thou truly."

The woman said to him, "Sir, I perceive that thou art
a prophet. Our fathers worshipped in this mountain; and
ye say, that in Jerusalem is the place where men ought
to worship." Jesus said, "Woman, believe me, the hour
cometh, when ye shall neither in this mountain, nor yet
at Jerusalem, worship the father. Ye worship ye know
not what: we know what we worship: for salvation is of
the Jews. But the hour cometh, and now is, when the
true worshippers shall worship the Father in spirit and
in truth: for the Father seeketh such to worship him. God
is a Spirit: and they that worship him must worship him
in spirit and in truth." The woman said to him, "I know
that Messias cometh, which is called Christ: When he is
come, he will tell us all things." Jesus said, "I that speak
unto thee am he."

As he was speaking his disciples came up and were surprised that he talked with the woman, yet no one said,
"What seekest thou?" or "Why talkest thou with her?"

The woman left her water-pot and went into the city
and said to the people, "Come, see a man, which told me
all things that ever I did: is not this the Christ?" Then
they left the city and went to him.

In the meantime his disciples urged him, "Master, eat."
But he replied to them, "I have meat to eat that ye know

not of." The disciples said to each other, "Hath any man brought him ought to eat?" Jesus said to them, "My meat is to do the will of him that sent me, and to finish his work. Say not ye, There are yet four months, and then cometh harvest? Behold, I say unto you, lift up your eyes, and look on the fields; for they are white already to harvest. And he that reapeth receiveth wages, and gathereth fruit unto life eternal: that both he that soweth and he that reapeth may rejoice together. And herein is that saying true, One soweth, and another reapeth. I sent you to reap that whereon ye bestowed no labour: other men laboured, and ye are entered into their labours."

Many of the Samaritans believed on him because the woman had said, "He told me all that ever I did." So the Samaritans urged him to visit with them, and he did for two days. Many more believed when they heard him speak and they said to the woman, "Now we believe, not because of thy saying: for we have heard him ourselves, and know that this is indeed the Christ, the Saviour of the world.

Meanwhile Herod had arrested John and put him in prison. When Jesus heard about it, he came to Galilee, preaching the good news of the kingdom of God and saying, "The time is fulfilled, and the kingdom of God is at hand: repent ye, and believe the gospel." The Galilaeans welcomed him because they were at the feast in Jerusalem and had seen all the things he did. There went out news about him in all the surrounding countryside. He taught in their synagogues and was praised by all. *Jesus Departs Into Galilee*

There was a nobleman in Capernaum whose son was sick. When he heard that Jesus had come from Judea to Galilee, he went and earnestly requested him to come and heal his son who was at the point of death. Jesus said to him, "Except ye see signs and wonders, ye will not believe." The nobleman said, "Sir, come down ere my child die." Jesus replied to him, "Go thy way; *The Nobleman's Son Healed*

| 29

thy son liveth." The man believed what Jesus spoke to
him and he started back home.

As he was on the way, his servants met him, saying,
"Thy son liveth." He inquired the hour when the boy
began to get better. They told him, "Yesterday at the
seventh hour the fever left him." The father knew that
it was at that very time when Jesus had said, "Thy son
liveth," and he and all his household believed.

*The Rejection
at Nazareth*

Jesus went from there to Nazareth, where he
had grown up, and his disciples were with him. As he
customarily did, he went to the synagogue on the sabbath day, and he stood to read. There was given to him
the book of the Prophet Isaiah. He opened the book and
found the place where it was written,

"The Spirit of the Lord is upon me,
Because he hath anointed me to preach the gospel to the
    poor;
He hath sent me to heal the brokenhearted,
To preach deliverance to the captives,
And recovering of sight to the blind,
To set at liberty them that are bruised,
To preach the acceptable year of the Lord."

He closed the book, handed it back to the minister and
sat down. The eyes of all those in the synagogue were
fixed on him.

He said to them, "This day is this scripture fulfilled in
your ears." All those present heard him and wondered
at the words which he spoke. Some were astonished and
said, "From whence hath this man these things? and
what wisdom is this which is given unto him, that even
such mighty works are wrought by his hands? Is not
this the carpenter, the son of Mary, the brother of James,
and Joses, and of Juda, and Simon? And are not his sisters
here with us?" They took offense at him. But Jesus said
to them, "No prophet is accepted in his own country.
But I tell you of a truth, many widows were in Israel in

the days of Elias, when the heaven was shut up three years and six months, when great famine was throughout all the land; but unto none of them was Elias sent, save Sarepta, a city of Sidon, unto a woman that was a widow. And many lepers were in Israel in the time of Eliseus the prophet; and none of them was cleansed, saving Naaman the Syrian."

This infuriated all the people in the synagogue and they carried him out of the city to the top of the hill on which the city was built, intending to throw him down head first. But he passed through the middle of them and went on his way. He could not do any mighty works there, except he did lay his hands upon a few sick people and healed them. He was amazed at their unbelief. He went around in the villages, teaching.

# THE YEAR
# OF POPULARITY

✠ *The Second Year of Christ's Ministry*

*Fishers of
Men*

Leaving Nazareth, Jesus went and settled in Capernaum on the Sea of Galilee. One day, as the people pushed around him to hear the word of God, he was standing by the shore of this lake. He saw two boats at the shore, but the fishermen were out washing their nets. He got into one of the boats, which belonged to Simon, and asked him to push out a little way from the land. Then he sat down and taught the people from the boat.

When he had finished speaking, he said to Simon, "Launch out into the deep, and let down your nets for a draught." Simon replied to him, "Master, we have toiled all the night, and have taken nothing: nevertheless at thy word I will let down the net." When they had done this, they caught so large a number of fish that their nets broke. They waved to their partners in the other ship to come and help them. They filled both the ships so full that they began to sink. When Simon Peter saw it, he fell down at Jesus' knees and said, "Depart from me; for I am a sinful man, O Lord!" He was amazed at the large catch which they had taken, as also were James and John, the sons of Zebedee, who were his partners. Jesus said to Simon, "Fear not; from henceforth thou shalt catch men." And when they had landed their ships, they left everything and followed him.

They went to Capernaum and on the Sabbath day he went into the synagogue and taught. The people were astonished at his teachings, for he taught with authority and not like the scribes. In the synagogue there was a man with an evil spirit. He cried out, "Let us alone; what have we to do with thee, thou Jesus of Nazareth? art thou come to destroy us? I know thee who thou art, the Holy One of God." Jesus rebuked him, "Hold thy peace, and come out of him." When the unclean spirit had thrown the man into a convulsion, he came out of him. The people were amazed and talked among themselves, saying, "What thing is this? what new doctrine is this? for with authority commandeth he even the unclean spirits, and they do obey him." Immediately his fame spread throughout the region around Galilee.

*Christ Teaches in Capernaum*

When they came out of the synagogue, they immediately went to the house of Simon and Andrew, with James and John with them. Simon's mother-in-law was in bed sick with a fever. They told him about it right away. He went to her, took her by the hand, and lifted her up. Immediately the fever left her and she began to look after their needs.

*Simon's Wife's Mother*

In the afternoon, at sunset, they brought to him all those who were sick and those who were possessed by evil spirits, and the people gathered around the door. He healed many of various sicknesses, cast out many evil spirits, but would not let the spirits speak because they knew him.

The next morning he got up long before daylight and went out to a solitary place to pray. Simon, and the others with him, followed. When they found him they said, "All men seek for thee." He said to them, "I must preach the kingdom of God to other cities also; for therefore am I sent."

*A Leper
Healed*

It happened that, when he was in a certain city, a leper came, knelt before him and begged, "If thou wilt, thou canst make me clean." Jesus was moved with compassion, put out his hand and touched him and said, "I will; be thou clean." As soon as he had spoken the leprosy left the man and he was healed. Then he instructed him and sent him away with the words, "See thou tell no man; but go thy way, and shew thyself to the priest, and offer the gift that Moses commanded, for a testimony unto them." But he went and began to tell everybody what had happened with the result that Jesus could not go into the city, but stayed out in the country. Even so people came to him from every side.

*The Man
Taken With a
Palsy*

After several days he went into Capernaum again, and it was told around that he was in the house. Quickly so many gathered together there was not room in the house for them, or even about the door. The people had come from every town of Galilee, and from Judea and Jerusalem, including Pharisees and doctors of the law. He preached to them and the power of the Lord was present to heal them. Some men brought a man on a bed who had palsy. They tried to find a way to get into the house to lay the man before Jesus. Because of the crowd, they could not get in so they went up on top of the house and let him down on his bed through the roof in front of Jesus. When he saw their faith, he said to him, "Man, thy sins are forgiven thee."

The scribes and Pharisees began to say among themselves, "Who is this which speaketh blasphemies? Who can forgive sins, but God alone?" When Jesus understood their thoughts, he answered, "What reason ye in your hearts? Whether is easier, to say, Thy sins be forgiven thee; or to say, Rise up and walk? But that ye may know that the Son of man hath power upon earth to forgive sins, I say unto thee, Arise, and take up thy couch, and go into thine house." Immediately he got up in front of them, picked up his bed and went home.

praising God. They were amazed and they praised God and fearfully exclaimed, "We have seen strange things to-day."

He went down to the seaside, the multitude *The Call of* came to him and he taught them. As he walked by, he *Matthew* saw Levi (also called Matthew), the son of Alphaeus, collecting taxes. He said to him, "Follow me," and he got up and followed him.

While Jesus was eating in Levi's house, many tax collectors and sinners sat with Jesus and his disciples. When the scribes and Pharisees saw him eating with these unrighteous people, they said to his disciples, "Why eateth your Master with publicans and sinners?" When Jesus heard what they said, he replied, "They that are whole need not a physician; but they that are sick. I am not come to call the righteous, but sinners to repentance."

They said to him, "Why do the disciples of *On Fasting* John fast often, and make prayers, and likewise the disciples of the Pharisees; but thine eat and drink?" He said to them, "Can ye make the children of the bridechamber fast, while the bridegroom is with them? But the days will come, when the bridegroom shall be taken away from them, and then shall they fast in those days."

Then he spoke a parable to them, "No man putteth a piece of a new garment upon an old; if otherwise, then both the new maketh a rent, and the piece that was taken out of the new agreeth not with the old. And no man putteth new wine into old bottles; else the new wine will burst the bottles, and be spilled, and the bottles shall perish. But new wine must be put into new bottles; and both are preserved. No man also having drunk old wine straightway desireth new: for he saith, The old is better."

Later on there was a Jewish feast and Jesus *The Man* went to Jerusalem. There is a pool by the sheep market *Healed at the* at Jerusalem, called Bethesda. It has five porches on *Pool of Be-* which lay a large number of sick people—blind, crippled, *thesda* paralyzed—waiting for the water to move. At certain

| 35

times an angel comes and stirs up the water. Then whoever gets into the water first, after it becomes calm, is healed of whatever sickness he has.

One man had been there for thirty-eight years. When Jesus saw him and learned that he had been there so long, he said to him, "Wilt thou be made whole?" The sick man answered, "Sir, I have no man, when the water is troubled, to put me into the pool: but while I am coming, another steppeth down before me." Jesus said to him, "Rise, take up thy bed, and walk." Immediately the man was healed, picked up his bed and walked.

This was on the Sabbath day. The Jews said to the man who had been healed, "It is the sabbath day: it is not lawful for thee to carry thy bed." He answered them, "He that made me whole, the same said unto me, Take up thy bed, and walk." Then they asked him, "What man is that which said unto thee, Take up thy bed, and walk?" But the healed man did not know who it was. for Jesus had slipped away and the place was crowded. Later Jesus found the man he had healed in the temple and said to him, "Behold, thou art made whole: sin no more, lest a worse thing come unto thee." The man left and told the Jews that it was Jesus who had cured him. Then the Jews began to persecute Jesus and tried to kill him, because he had done this on the Sabbath day. Jesus replied to them, "My Father worketh hitherto, and I work." This caused the Jews to try harder to kill him because not only had he broken the Sabbath, but by saying that God was his father, he was making himself equal with God.

Jesus replied to them, "Verily, verily, I say unto you, the Son can do nothing of himself, but what he seeth the Father do: for what things soever he doeth, these also doeth the Son likewise. For the Father loveth the Son, and sheweth him all things that himself doeth: and he will shew him greater works than these, that ye may marvel. For as the Father raiseth up the dead, and quickeneth them; even so the Son quickeneth whom he will. For the Father judgeth no man, but hath committed all judgment unto the son: that all men should honour the Son, even as they honour the Father. He that honoureth not the Son honoureth not the Father which hath sent him. Verily, verily, I say unto you, he that heareth my word, and believeth on him that sent me, hath everlasting life, and shall not come into condemnation; but is passed from death unto life. Verily, verily, I say unto you, the hour is coming, and now is, when the dead shall hear the voice of the Son of God: and they that hear shall live. For as the Father hath life in himself; so hath he given to the Son to have life in himself; and hath given him authority to execute judgment also, because he is the Son of man. Marvel not at this: for the hour is coming, in which all that are in the graves shall hear his voice, and shall come forth; they that have done good, unto the resurrection of life; and they that have done evil, unto the resurrection of damnation.

"I can of mine own self do nothing: as I hear, I judge: and my judgment is just; because I seek not mine own will, but the will of the Father which hath sent me. If I bear witness of myself, my witness is not true. There is another that beareth witness of me; and I know that the witness which he witnesseth of me is true. Ye sent unto John, and he bare witness unto the truth. But I receive not testimony from man: but these things I say, that ye might be saved. He was a burning and a shining light: and ye were willing for a season to rejoice in his light. But I have greater witness than that of John: for the works which the Father hath given me to finish, the same works that I do, bear witness of me, that the Father hath sent me. And the Father himself, which hath sent me, hath borne witness of me. Ye have neither heard his voice at any time, nor seen his shape. And ye have not his word abiding in you: for whom he hath sent, him ye believe not. Search the scriptures; for in them ye ] 37 think ye have eternal life: and they are they which testify of me. And ye will not come to me, that ye might have life. I receive not honour from men. But I know you, that ye have not the love of God in you. I am come in my Father's name, and ye receive me not: if another shall come in his own name, him ye will receive. How can ye believe, which receive honour one of another, and seek not the honour that cometh from God only? Do not think that I will accuse you to the Father: there is one that accuseth you, even Moses, in whom ye trust. For had ye believed Moses, ye would have believed me: for he wrote of me. But if ye believe not his writings, how shall ye believe my words?"

*The Lord of
the Sabbath*

And on the Sabbath day Jesus walked through cornfields. His disciples were hungry and began to pull some ears of corn to eat. When the Pharisees saw it, they said to him, "Behold, thy disciples do that which is not lawful to do upon the sabbath day." He said to them, "Have ye not read what David did, when he was an hungered and they that were with him; how he entered into the house of God, and did eat the shewbread, which was not lawful for him to eat, neither for them which were with him, but only for the priests? Or have ye not read in the law, how that on the sabbath days the priests in the temple profane the sabbath, and are blameless? But I say unto you that in this place is one greater than the temple. But if ye had known what this meaneth, I will have mercy, and not sacrifice, ye would not have condemned the guiltless."

And he added, "The sabbath was made for man, and not man for the sabbath: therefore the Son of man is Lord also of the sabbath."

*The With-
ered Hand
Healed*

It happened on another Sabbath that he went into the synagogue and taught. Present was a man whose right hand was withered. The scribes and Pharisees watched to see if he would heal on the Sabbath so that they might have an accusation against him. He understood their thoughts and said to the man with the

38 |

withered hand, "Rise up, and stand forth in the midst."
The man rose and came forward. Then Jesus said to them,
"I will ask you one thing; Is it lawful on the sabbath days
to do good, or to do evil? to save life, or to destroy it?"
Looking around at all of them, he said to the man,
"Stretch forth thine hand." He did so and his hand was
restored like his other one. They were filled with rage
and the Pharisees plotted with the Herodians as to how
they might destroy him.

Jesus went throughout Galilee, teaching in *Prophecy of*
their synagogues, preaching about the kingdom and heal- *Isaiah*
ing all types of sickness and disease among the people.
News about him went all over Syria, and people with all
kinds of sicknesses were brought to him and he healed
them. Large numbers of people followed him from
Galilee, Decapolis, Jerusalem, Judea, and from beyond
the Jordan.

At this time the Pharisees counseled as to how they
might destroy him. When Jesus found it out, he left there.
Many people followed him. He healed them and instructed
them not to make him known. Thus the words of the
prophet Isaiah were fulfilled:

> "Behold my servant, whom I have chosen;
> My beloved, in whom my soul is well pleased:
> I will put my spirit upon him,
> And he shall shew judgment to the Gentiles.
> He shall not strive, nor cry;
> Neither shall any man hear his voice in the streets.
> A bruised reed shall he not break,
> And smoking flax shall he not quench,
> Till he send forth judgment unto victory.
> And in his name shall the Gentiles trust."

During these days, he went out on a mountain- *Choosing The*
side to pray. He prayed all night, and when it was day *Twelve*
he called around him his disciples, and of them he chose
twelve, whom also he named apostles: Simon (whom he
also named Peter) and Andrew his brother, James and

| 39

John, Philip and Bartholomew, Matthew and Thomas, James, the son of Alphaeus, and Simon called Zelotes, and Judas, the brother of James, and Judas Iscariot, which also was the traitor.

He came down with them and stood on some level ground. His disciples and a large multitude of people from Judea, Jerusalem and from the sea coast of Tyre and Sidon were there with him. They came to hear him and to be healed of their diseases. They were healed and the whole multitude tried to touch him.

*The Sermon on the Mount* Seeing the multitude, he went up on the side of the mountain. After he had sat down, his disciples came to where he was and he began to teach them:

"Blessed are the poor in spirit: for theirs is the kingdom of heaven.

"Blessed are they that mourn: for they shall be comforted.

"Blessed are the meek: for they shall inherit the earth.

"Blessed are they which do hunger and thirst after righteousness: for they shall be filled.

"Blessed are the merciful: for they shall obtain mercy.

"Blessed are the pure in heart: for they shall see God.

"Blessed are the peacemakers: for they shall be called the children of God.

"Blessed are they which are persecuted for righteousness' sake: for theirs is the kingdom of heaven.

"Blessed are ye when men shall revile you, and persecute you, and shall say all manner of evil against you falsely, for my sake. Rejoice, and be exceeding glad: for great is your reward in heaven: for so persecuted they the prophets which were before you.

"Ye are the salt of the earth: but if the salt have lost his savour, wherewith shall it be salted? it is thenceforth good for nothing, but to be cast out, and to be trodden under foot of men. Ye are the light of the world. A city that is set on an hill cannot be hid. Neither do men light a

40 |

candle, and put it under a bushel, but on a candlestick; and it giveth light unto all that are in the house. Let your light so shine before men, that they may see your good works, and glorify your Father which is in heaven.

"Think not that I am come to destroy the law, or the prophets: I am not come to destroy, but to fulfil. For verily I say unto you, Till heaven and earth pass, one jot or one tittle shall in no wise pass from the law, till all be fulfilled. Whosoever therefore shall break one of these least commandments, and shall teach men so, he shall be called the least in the kingdom of heaven: but whosoever shall do and teach them, the same shall be called great in the kingdom of heaven. For I say unto you, That except your righteousness shall exceed the righteousness of the scribes and Pharisees, ye shall in no case enter into the kingdom of heaven.

"Ye have heard that it was said by them of old time, Thou shalt not kill, and whosoever shall kill shall be in danger of the judgment: But I say unto you, That whosoever is angry with his brother without a cause shall be in danger of the judgment: and whosoever shall say to his brother, Raca, shall be in danger of the council: but whosoever shall say, Thou fool, shall be in danger of hell fire. Therefore if thou bring thy gift to the altar, and there rememberest that thy brother hath aught against thee; Leave there thy gift before the altar, and go thy way; first be reconciled to thy brother, and then come and offer thy gift. Agree with thine adversary quickly, while thou art in the way with him; lest at any time the adversary deliver thee to the judge, and the judge deliver thee to the officer, and thou be cast into prison. Verily I say unto thee, Thou shalt by no means come out thence, till thou hast paid the uttermost farthing.

"Ye have heard that it was said by them of old time, Thou shalt not commit adultery: But I say unto you, That whosoever looketh on a woman to lust after her hath committed adultery with her already in his heart.

| 41

And if thy right eye offend thee, pluck it out, and cast it from thee: for it is profitable for thee that one of thy members should perish, and not that thy whole body should be cast into hell. And if thy right hand offend thee, cut it off, and cast it from thee: for it is profitable for thee that one of thy members should perish, and not that thy whole body should be cast into hell. It hath been said, Whosoever shall put away his wife, let him give her a writing of divorcement: But I say unto you, That whosoever shall put away his wife, saving for the cause of fornication, causeth her to commit adultery: and whosoever shall marry her that is divorced committeth adultery.

"Again, ye have heard that it hath been said by them of old time, Thou shall not forswear thyself, but shalt perform unto the Lord thine oaths: But I say unto you, Swear not at all; neither by heaven; for it is God's throne: Nor by the earth; for it is his footstool: neither by Jerusalem; for it is the city of the great King. Neither shalt thou swear by thy head, because thou canst not make one hair white or black. But let your communication be, Yea, yea; Nay, nay: for whatsoever is more than these cometh of evil.

"Ye have heard that it hath been said, An eye for an eye, and a tooth for a tooth: But I say unto you, That ye resist not evil: but whosoever shall smite thee on thy right cheek, turn to him the other also. And if any man will sue thee at the law, and take away thy coat, let him have thy cloak also. And whosoever shall compel thee to go a mile, go with him twain. Give to him that asketh thee, and from him that would borrow of thee turn not thou away.

"Ye have heard that it hath been said, Thou shalt love thy neighbor, and hate thine enemy. But I say unto you, Love your enemies, bless them that curse you, do good to them that hate you, and pray for them which despitefully use you, and persecute you; That ye may be the children of your Father which is in heaven: for he maketh his sun to rise on the evil and on the good, and sendeth rain on the just and on the unjust. For if ye love them which love you, what reward have ye? do not even the publicans the same? And if ye salute your brethren only, what do ye more than others? do not even the publicans so? Be ye therefore perfect, even as your Father which is in heaven is perfect.

"Take heed that ye do not your alms before men, to be seen of them: otherwise ye have no reward of your Father which is in heaven. Therefore when thou doest thine alms, do not sound a trumpet before thee, as the hypocrites do in the synagogues and in the streets, that they may have glory of men. Verily I say unto you, They have their reward. But when thou doest alms, let not thy left hand know what thy right hand doeth: That thine alms may be in secret: and thy Father which seeth in secret himself shall reward thee openly.

"And when thou prayest, thou shalt not be as the hypocrites are: for they love to pray standing in the synagogues and in the corners of the streets, that they may be seen of men. Verily I say unto you, They have their reward. But thou, when thou prayest, enter into thy closet, and when thou hast shut thy door, pray to thy Father which is in secret; and thy Father which seeth in secret shall reward thee openly. But when ye pray, use not vain repetitions, as the heathen do: for they think that they shall be heard for their much speaking. Be not ye therefore like unto them: for your Father knoweth what things ye have need of, before ye ask him. After this manner therefore pray ye: Our Father which art in heaven, Hallowed be thy name. Thy kingdom come. Thy will be done in earth, as it is in heaven. Give us this day our daily bread. And forgive us our debts, as we forgive our debtors. And lead us not into temptation, but deliver us from evil: For thine is the kingdom, and the power, and the glory, for ever. Amen. For if ye forgive men their trespasses, your heavenly Father will also forgive you: But if ye forgive not men their trespasses, neither will your Father forgive your trespasses.

"Moreover when ye fast, be not, as the hypocrites, of

a sad countenance: for they disfigure their faces, that they
may appear unto men to fast. Verily I say unto you,
They have their reward. But thou, when thou fastest,
anoint thine head, and wash thy face; That thou appear
not unto men to fast, but unto thy Father which is in
secret and thy Father which seeth in secret shall reward
thee openly.

"Lay not up for yourselves treasures upon earth, where
moth and rust doth corrupt, and where thieves break
through and steal: But lay up for yourselves treasures in
heaven, where neither moth nor rust doth corrupt, and
where thieves do not break through nor steal: For where
your treasure is, there will your heart be also. The light
of the body is the eye: if therefore thine eye be single, thy
whole body shall be full of light. But if thine eye be evil,
thy whole body shall be full of darkness. If therefore the
light that is in thee be darkness, how great is that darkness!

"No man can serve two masters: for either he will
hate the one, and love the other; or else he will hold to
the one, and despise the other. Ye cannot serve God and
mammon. Therefore I say unto you, Take no thought for
your life, what ye shall eat, or what ye shall drink; nor yet
for your body, what ye shall put on. Is not the life more
than meat, and the body than raiment? Behold the fowls
of the air: for they sow not, neither do they reap, nor
gather into barns; yet your heavenly Father feedeth them.
Are ye not much better than they? Which of you by
taking thought can add one cubit unto his stature? And
why take ye thought for raiment? Consider the lilies of
the field, how they grow; they toil not, neither do they
spin: And yet I say unto you, That even Solomon in all
his glory was not arrayed like one of these. Wherefore,
if God so clothe the grass of the field, which today is,
and tomorrow is cast into the oven, shall he not much
more clothe you, O ye of little faith? Therefore take no
thought, saying What shall we eat? or, What shall we
drink? or, Wherewithal shall we be clothed? (For after

all these things do the Gentiles seek:) for your heavenly Father knoweth that ye have need of all these things. But seek ye first the kingdom of God, and his righteousness; and all these things shall be added unto you. Take therefore no thought for the morrow: for the morrow shall take thought for the things of itself. Sufficient unto the day is the evil thereof.

"Judge not, that ye be not judged. For with what judgment ye judge, ye shall be judged: and with what measure ye mete, it shall be measured to you again. And why beholdest thou the mote that is in thy brother's eye, but considerest not the beam that is in thine own eye? Or how wilt thou say to thy brother, Let me pull out the mote out of thine eye; and, behold, a beam is in thine own eye? Thou hypocrite, first cast out the beam out of thine own eye; and then shalt thou see clearly to cast out the mote out of thy brother's eye.

"Give not that which is holy unto the dogs, neither cast ye your pearls before swine, lest they trample them under their feet, and turn again and rend you.

"Ask, and it shall be given you; seek, and ye shall find; knock, and it shall be opened unto you: For every one that asketh receiveth; and he that seeketh findeth; and to him that knocketh it shall be opened. Or what man is there of you, whom if his son ask bread, will he give him a stone? Of if he ask a fish, will he give him a serpent? If ye then, being evil, know how to give good gifts unto your children, how much more shall your Father which is in heaven give good things to them that ask him? Therefore all things whatsoever ye would that men should do to you, do ye even so to them: for this is the law and the prophets.

"Enter ye in at the strait gate: for wide is the gate, and broad is the way, that leadeth to destruction, and many there be which go in thereat: Because strait is the gate, and narrow is the way, which leadeth unto life, and few there be that find it.

"Beware of false prophets, which come to you in sheep's clothing, but inwardly they are ravening wolves. Ye shall know them by their fruits. Do men gather grapes of thorns, or figs of thistles? Even so every good tree bringeth forth good fruit; but a corrupt tree bringeth forth evil fruit. A good tree cannot bring forth evil fruit, neither can a corrupt tree bring forth good fruit. Every tree that bringeth not forth good fruit is hewn down, and cast into the fire. Wherefore by their fruits ye shall know them.

"Not every one that saith unto me, Lord, Lord, shall enter into the kingdom of heaven; but he that doeth the will of my Father which is in heaven. Many will say to me in that day, Lord, Lord, have we not prophesied in thy name? and in thy name have cast out devils? and in thy name done many wonderful works? And then will I profess unto them, I never knew you: depart from me, ye that work iniquity.

"Therefore whosoever heareth these sayings of mine, and doeth them, I will liken him unto a wise man, which built his house upon a rock: And the rain descended, and the floods came, and the winds blew, and beat upon that house; and it fell not: for it was founded upon a rock. And every one that heareth these sayings of mine, and doeth them not, shall be likened unto a foolish man, which built his house upon the sand: And the rain descended, and the floods came, and the winds blew, and beat upon that house; and it fell: and great was the fall of it."

When Jesus had finished speaking, the people were astonished for he taught with authority instead of the wishy-washy manner of the scribes.

*The Centu-*
*rion's Faith*

After he had finished teaching the people, he went to Capernaum. A centurion there had a servant who was of great worth to him. The servant was sick of the palsy and about to die. When he heard of Jesus, he sent the Jewish elders to ask him to come and heal his servant. When they came to Jesus, immediately they urged him to do this, saying the centurion was a worthy man, "For he loveth our nation, and he hath built us a synagogue."

Jesus went with them. When he got near the house, the centurion sent friends to him to say, "Lord, trouble not thyself; for I am not worthy that thou shouldest enter under my roof: wherefore neither thought I myself worthy to come unto thee: but say in a word, and my servant shall be healed. For I also am a man set under authority, having under me soldiers, and I say unto one, Go, and he goeth; and to another, Come, and he cometh; and to my servant, Do this, and he doeth it."

When Jesus heard what they had said, he was surprised and turning around, said to the people that followed him, "I say unto you, I have not found so great faith, no, not in Israel." Those who had been sent returned to the house and found the servant well, who had been sick.

The next day he went to a city called Nain. *The Widow* Many of his disciples went with him, along with many *of Nain's Son* other people. When he came near to the gate of the city, there was a funeral procession of a man who was the only son of a widow. Many people were with the mother in the procession. When Jesus saw her, he had compassion on her, and said to her, "Weep not." He came and touched the casket and those who were carrying it stood still. He said, "Young man, I say unto thee, Arise." The man who was dead sat up and began to speak. He then gave him to his mother.

The people felt a deep reverence and they praised God, saying, "A great prophet is risen up among us," and, "God hath visited his people." The account of what he had done was told throughout Judea and the surrounding area.

John's disciples told him the things Jesus had *Messengers* done. John called two of his disciples and sent them to *From John* Jesus, asking, "Art thou he that should come, or look we *the Baptist* for another?" At that very time Jesus cured many of their sicknesses and gave sight to many who were blind. Jesus answered them, "Go your way and tell John what things ye have seen and heard; how that the blind see, the lame walk, the lepers are cleansed, the deaf hear, the dead are raised, to the poor the gospel is preached. And blessed is he, whosoever shall not be offended in me."

When the messengers of John had gone, he began to speak to the people concerning John, "What went ye out into the wilderness for to see? A reed shaken with the wind? But what went ye out for to see? A man clothed in soft raiment? Behold, they which are gorgeously apparelled, and live delicately, are in kings' courts. But what went ye out for to see? A prophet? Yea, I say unto you, and much more than a prophet. This is he, of whom it is written,

Behold, I send my messenger before thy face,
Which shall prepare thy way before thee.

For I say unto you, Among those that are born of women there is not a greater prophet than John the Baptist: but he that is least in the kingdom of God is greater than he." And all the people that heard Him, and the publicans, justified God, being baptized with the baptism of John. But the Pharisees and lawyers rejected the counsel of God against themselves, being not baptized of him.

And the Lord said, "Whereunto then shall I liken the men of this generation? and to what are they like? They are like unto children sitting in the marketplace, and calling one to another, and saying, We have piped unto you, and ye have not danced; we have mourned to you, and ye have not wept. For John the Baptist came neither eating bread nor drinking wine; and ye say, He hath a devil. The Son of man is come eating and drinking; and ye say, Behold a gluttonous man, and a winebibber, a friend of publicans and sinners! But wisdom is justified of all her children."

48 |

Then he began to denounce the cities in which most

of his mighty works had been done, because they had not repented. "Woe unto thee, Chorazin! woe unto thee, Bethsaida! for if the mighty works which were done in you had been done in Tyre and Sidon, they would have repented long ago in sack-cloth and ashes. But I say unto you, it shall be more tolerable for Tyre and Sidon at the day of judgment, than for you. And thou, Capernaum, which art exalted unto heaven, shalt be brought down to hell: for if the mighty works, which have been done in thee, had been done in Sodom, it would have remained until this day. But I say unto you, That it shall be more tolerable for the land of Sodom in the day of judgment, than for thee."

Then Jesus spoke these words: "I thank thee, O Father, Lord of heaven and earth, because thou hast hid these things from the wise and prudent, and hast revealed them unto babes. Even so, Father; for so it seemed good in thy sight. All things are delivered unto me of my Father: and no man knoweth the Son, but the Father; neither knoweth any man the Father, save the Son, and he to whomsoever the Son will reveal him. Come unto me, all ye that labour and are heavy laden, and I will give you rest. Take my yoke upon you, and learn of me; for I am meek and lowly in heart: and ye shall find rest unto your souls. For my yoke is easy, and my burden is light."

One of the Pharisees invited him to dinner. He went to the Pharisee's house and sat down at the table. A sinful woman in the city, when she learned that Jesus was having dinner in the Pharisee's house, brought an alabaster box of ointment. She, weeping, took her place near him at his feet. She began to wash his feet with tears and to wipe them with the hair of her head, and she kissed his feet and anointed them with ointment.

*Christ
Anointed at
the Pharisee's
House*

When the Pharisee who had invited Jesus saw it, he said to himself, "This man, if he were a prophet, would have known who and what manner of woman this is

that toucheth him: for she is a sinner." Jesus said to him
"Simon, I have somewhat to say unto thee." He replied
"Master, say on." "There was a certain creditor which
had two debtors: the one owed five hundred pence, and
the other fifty. And when they had nothing to pay, he
frankly forgave them both. Tell me therefore, which
of them will love him most?" Simon answered and said
"I suppose that he, to whom he forgave most." And he
said unto him, "Thou hast rightly judged."

*Women Min-
ister Unto
Christ*

He then looked at the woman and said to
Simon, "Seest thou this woman? I entered into thine
house, thou gavest me no water for my feet: but she hath
washed my feet with tears, and wiped them with the
hairs of her head. Thou gavest me no kiss: but this woman
since the time I came in hath not ceased to kiss my feet.
My head with oil thou didst not anoint: but this woman
hath anointed my feet with ointment. Wherefore I say
unto thee, Her sins, which are many, are forgiven; for
she loved much: but to whom little is forgiven, the same
loveth little." And he said unto her, "Thy sins are forgiven!" And they that sat at meat with him began to
say within themselves, "Who is this that forgiveth sin
also?" And he said to the woman, "Thy faith hath saved
thee; go in peace."

Afterward he went to all the cities and villages, preaching the good news of the Kingdom of God. The twelve
were with him and certain women who had been healed
by him—Mary called Magdalene, out of whom seven
devils had come; Joanna the wife of Herod's steward
Chuza; Susanna, and many others, who shared with him
their food.

*Blind Demo-
niac Healed.
The Unpar-
donable Sin*

They went into a house and the crowds of
people gathered so that they had no chance to eat. When
his family heard about it, they went to take charge of
him because people were saying, "He is beside himself."

There one was brought to him who was possessed of
a devil and also was blind and dumb. Jesus healed him

and he both spoke and saw. The people were amazed and said, "Is not this the son of David?" When the Pharisees heard it, they said, "This fellow doth not cast out devils, but by Beelzebub the prince of devils." Jesus understood their thoughts and said to them, "How can Satan cast out Satan? Every kingdom divided against itself is brought to desolation; and every city or house divided against itself shall not stand: and if Satan cast out Satan, he is divided against himself; how shall then his kingdom stand? And if I by Beelzebub cast out devils, by whom do your children cast them out? therefore they shall be your judges. But if I cast out devils by the Spirit of God, then the kingdom of God is come unto you. Or else how can one enter into a strong man's house, and spoil his goods, except he first bind the strong man? and then he will spoil his house. He that is not with me is against me; and he that gathereth not with me scattereth abroad. Wherefore I say unto you, All manner of sin and blasphemy shall be forgiven unto men: but the blasphemy against the Holy Ghost shall not be forgiven unto men. And whosoever speaketh a word against the Son of man, it shall be forgiven him: but whosoever speaketh against the Holy Ghost, it shall not be forgiven him, neither in this world, neither in the world to come. Either make the tree good, and his fruit good; or else make the tree corrupt, and his fruit corrupt: for the tree is known by his fruit. O generation of vipers, how can ye, being evil, speak good things? for out of the abundance of the heart the mouth speaketh. A good man out of the good treasure of the heart bringeth forth good things: and an evil man out of the evil treasure bringeth forth evil things, for of the abundance of the heart his mouth speaketh. But I say unto you, That every idle word that men shall speak, they shall give account thereof in the day of judgment. For by thy words thou shalt be justified, and by thy words thou shalt be condemned."

Then certain ones among the scribes and Pharisees said, "Master, we would see a sign from thee." He replied to them, "An evil and adulterous generation seeketh after a sign; and there shall no sign be given to it, but the sign of the prophet Jonas: for as Jonas was three days and three nights in the whale's belly; so shall the Son of man be three days and three nights in the heart of the earth. The men of Nineveh shall rise in judgment with this generation, and shall condemn it: because they repented at the preaching of Jonas; and, behold, a greater than Jonas is here. The queen of the south shall rise up in the judgment with this generation, and shall condemn it: for she came from the uttermost parts of the earth to hear the wisdom of Solomon; and, behold, a greater than Solomon is here. When the unclean spirit is gone out of a man, he walketh through dry places, seeking rest, and findeth none. Then he saith I will return into my house from whence I came out; and when he is come, he findeth it empty, swept, and garnished. Then goeth he, and taketh with himself seven other spirits more wicked than himself, and they enter in and dwell there: and the last state of that man is worse than the first. Even so shall it be also unto this wicked generation."

*The True Kindred of Christ*

As he spoke these things, one of the women present said to him in a loud voice, "Blessed is the womb that bare thee, and the paps which thou hast sucked." He replied, "Rather, blessed are they that hear the word of God, and keep it."

While he was speaking, his mother and brothers came and stood outside, wishing to speak with him. Someone told him, "Behold, thy mother and thy brethren stand without, desiring to speak with thee." He replied to him, "Who is my mother? and who are my brethren?" He pointed to his disciples and said, "Behold my mother and my brethren! For whosoever shall do the will of my Father which is in heaven, the same is my brother, and sister, and mother."

That same day Jesus left the house and went *The Parable of* and sat down by the seaside. So many people gathered *the Sower* around him that he got into a ship, and all the people were on the shore. He taught them many things by parables. He said to them, "Harken; Behold, there went out a sower to sow: and it came to pass, as he sowed, some fell by the way side, and the fowls of the air came and devoured it up. And some fell on stony ground, where it had not much earth; and immediately it sprang up, because it had no depth of earth: but when the sun was up, it was scorched; and because it had no root, it withered away. And some fell among thorns, and the thorns grew up, and choked it, and it yielded no fruit. And the other fell on good ground, and did yield fruit that sprang up and increased; and brought forth, some thirty, and some sixty, and some an hundred." And he said to them, "He that hath ears to hear, let him hear."

When he was alone the disciples came and asked him, "Why speakest thou unto them in parables?" He answered, "Because it is given unto you to know the mysteries of the kingdom of heaven, but to them it is not given. For whosoever hath, to him shall be given, and he shall have more abundance: but whosoever hath not, from him shall be taken away even that he hath. Therefore speak I to them in parables: because they seeing see not; and hearing they hear not, neither do they understand. And in them is fulfilled the prophecy of Esaias, which saith,

By hearing ye shall hear, and shall not understand;
And seeing ye shall see, and shall not perceive:
For this people's heart is waxed gross,
And their ears are dull of hearing,
And their eyes they have closed;
Lest at any time they should see with their eyes,
And hear with their ears,
And should understand with their heart,

| 53

And should be converted,
And I should heal them.

But blessed are your eyes, for they see: and your ears, for they hear. For verily I say unto you, That many prophets and righteous men have desired to see those things which ye see, and have not seen them; and to hear those things which ye hear, and have not heard them." And he said to them, "Know ye not this parable? and how then will ye know all parables? The sower soweth the word. And these are they by the way side, where the word is sown; but when they have heard, Satan cometh immediately, and taketh away the word that was sown in their hearts. And these are they likewise which are sown on stony ground; who, when they have heard the word, immediately receive it with gladness; and have no root in themselves, and so endure but for a time: afterward, when affliction or persecution ariseth for the word's sake, immediately they are offended. And these are they which are sown among thorns; such as hear the word, and the cares of this world, and the deceitfulness of riches and the lusts of other things entering in, choke the word, and it becometh unfruitful. And these are they which are sown on good ground; such as hear the word, and receive it, and bring forth fruit, some thirtyfold, some sixty, and some an hundred.

*The Lighted Lamp*

"No man, when he hath lighted a candle, covereth it with a vessel, or putteth it under a bed; but setteth it on a candlestick, that they which enter in may see the light. For nothing is secret, that shall not be made manifest; neither any thing hid, that shall not be known and come abroad. Take heed therefore how ye hear."

*The Parable of the Tares*

He told them another parable: "The kingdom of heaven is likened unto a man which sowed good seed in his field: but while men slept, his enemy came and sowed tares among the wheat, and went his way. But when the blade was sprung up, and brought forth fruit, then appeared the tares also. So the servants of the householder came and said unto him, Sir, didst not thou sow good seed in thy field? from whence then hath it tares? He said unto them, An enemy hath done this. The servants said unto him, Wilt thou then that we go and gather them up? But he said, Nay; lest while ye gather up the tares, ye root up also the wheat with them. Let both grow together until the harvest: and in the time of harvest I will say to the reapers, Gather ye together first the tares, and bind them in bundles to burn them: but gather the wheat into my barn."

And he said, "So is the kingdom of God, as if *Secret Growth* a man should cast seed into the ground; and should sleep, *of the Seed* and rise night and day, and the seed should spring and grow up, he knoweth not how. For the earth bringeth forth fruit of herself; first the blade, then the ear, after that the full corn in the ear. But when the fruit is brought forth, immediately he putteth in the sickle, because the harvest is come."

Then he told them another parable: "The *Parable of the* kingdom of heaven is like to a grain of mustard seed, *Mustard Seed* which a man took, and sowed in his field: which indeed is the least of all seeds: but when it is grown, it is the greatest among herbs, and becometh a tree, so that the birds of the air come and lodge in the branches thereof."

Another parable he spoke to them: "The king- *The Leaven* dom of heaven is like unto leaven, which a woman took, and hid in three measures of meal, till the whole was leavened."

Jesus spoke all these things to the multitude in parables, and He had nothing to say to them except parables. Thus was fulfilled which was said by the prophet: "I will open my mouth in parables; I will utter things which have been kept secret from the foundation of the world."

Then Jesus sent the multitude away and went into the house. His disciples came to him and said, "Declare unto us the parable of the tares of the field." He answered them, "He that soweth the good seed is the Son of man; the field is the world; the good seed are the children of the kingdom; but the tares are the children of the wicked one; the enemy that sowed them is the devil; the harvest is the end of the world; and the reapers are the angels. As therefore the tares are gathered and burned in the fire; so shall it be in the end of this world. The Son of man shall send forth his angels, and they shall gather out of his kingdom all things that offend, and them which do iniquity; and shall cast them into a furnace of fire: there shall be wailing and gnashing of teeth. Then shall the righteous shine forth as the sun in the kingdom of their Father. Who hath ears to hear, let him hear.

*The Hidden Treasure*

"Again, the kingdom of heaven is like unto treasure hid in a field," the which when a man hath found, he hideth, and for joy thereof goeth and selleth all that he hath, and buyeth that field.

*The Pearl of Great Price*

"Again, the kingdom of heaven is like unto a merchant man, seeking goodly pearls: who, when he had found one pearl of great price, went and sold all that he had, and bought it.

*Parable of the Net*

Again, the kingdom of heaven is like unto a net, that was cast into the sea, and gathered of every kind: which, when it was full, they drew to shore, and sat down, and gathered the good into vessels, but cast the bad away. So shall it be at the end of the world: the angels shall come forth, and sever the wicked from among the just, and shall cast them into the furnace of fire: there shall be wailing and gnashing of teeth."

Jesus asked them, "Have ye understood all these things?" They said to him, "Yea, Lord." Then he said to them, "Therefore every scribe which is instructed unto the kingdom of heaven is like unto a man that is an householder, which bringeth forth out of his treasure things new and old."

When he had finished these parables, he left.

*Stilling the Tempest*

One day he went with his disciples on a ship and said to them, "Let us pass over unto the other side." They launched out. A strong wind rose and the waves filled the ship. He was in the rear of the ship, asleep on a cushion. They woke him and said, "Master, carest thou not that we perish?" He got up, rebuked the wind, and said to the sea, "Peace, be still!" The wind ceased and there was dead calm. He said to them, "Why are ye so fearful? how is it that ye have no faith?" They were very frightened and said to each other, "What manner of man is this, that even the wind and the sea obey him?"

They came to the other side of the sea to the Gadarenes' country. As soon as he came out of the ship, a man who lived in the cemetery, and who had an unclean spirit, met him. No one could bind him, not even with chains. He had often been bound with fetters and chains but he tore up the chains and broke the fetters into pieces. No one could subdue him. He spent his time, day and night, in the mountains and among the tombs, screaming and cutting himself with stones.

*The Legion of Devils Cast Out*

When he saw Jesus a long way off, he ran and knelt before him and shouted, "What have I to do with thee, Jesus, thou Son of the most high God? I adjure thee by God, that thou torment me not." For Jesus had said, "Come out of the man, thou unclean spirit!" He asked him, "What is thy name?" He replied, "My name is Legion: for we are many." He begged him not to send them out of the country.

There was a large herd of swine feeding near the mountains. The devils begged him, "Send us into the swine, that we may enter into them." Immediately Jesus let them go. The unclean spirits went and entered into the swine and the herd ran madly down a steep hill into the sea. There were about two thousand of them and they drowned in the sea.

Those who were looking after the swine ran and told in the city and country all that had happened. The whole city came out to meet Jesus. They went out to see what had been done. They came to Jesus and saw the man who had been possessed by the devil, sitting, clothed, and in his right mind. They were afraid. Those that had seen it told what had happened to the man and the swine. Then

| 57

the many people of the Gadarene country urged him to leave for they were overcome with fear.

When he got to the ship, the man, who had been possessed with the devil, begged to go with him. Jesus would not permit it, but said to him, "Go home to thy friends, and tell them how great things the Lord hath done for thee, and hath compassion on thee." He left and began to tell in Decapolis the great things Jesus had done for him, and everyone was amazed.

When Jesus had crossed over by ship to the other side, many people gathered around him on the shore. Jairus, one of the rulers of the synagogue, came up. When he saw Jesus he fell at his feet and pleaded with him, saying, "My little daughter lieth at the point of death: I pray thee, come and lay thy hands on her, that she may be healed; and she shall live."

*The Issue of Blood Healed*
Jesus went with him and many people followed. A certain woman who had had a hemorrhage for twelve years, though she had had treatment by many physicians and had spent all her money without getting any better, and instead had become worse, came among the crowd behind and touched his cloak; for she said, "If I may touch but his clothes, I shall be whole." Immediately the blood ceased and she felt inside herself that she had been healed of her sickness. Knowing that power had gone out of him, Jesus turned about in the crowd and asked, "Who touched my clothes?" His disciples said to him, "Thou seest the multitude thronging thee, and sayest thou, who touched me?" He looked around to see who had done this. The woman, fearful and trembling, knowing what had been done for her, came and fell down before him and told him the truth. He said to her, "Daughter, thy faith hath made thee whole; go in peace, and be whole of thy plague."

*Jairus' Daughter Raised*
While he was speaking, there came from the ruler of the synagogue's house one who said, "Thy daughter is dead: why troublest thou the Master any

further?" As soon as Jesus heard what had been said, he said to the ruler of the synagogue, "Fear not: believe only, and she shall be made whole." He allowed no one to follow him, except Peter, James, and John, the brother of James.

He came to the house of the ruler of the synagogue and saw the tumult brought on by those who greatly wept and wailed. When he was inside, he said to them, "Why make ye this ado, and weep? the damsel is not dead, but sleepeth." They laughed at him scornfully. He made them all get out; then he took the child's father and mother, and those who were with him, and went in the room where the girl was lying. He took her by the hand and said to her, "Talitha cumi," which means, "Damsel, I say unto thee, arise." Immediately the girl got up and walked—she was twelve years old. They were beside themselves with astonishment. He ordered them not to let any one know it and told them to give her something to eat.

*Two Blind Men and Dumb Demoniac Healed*

When Jesus had left there, he was followed by two blind men, who were crying out, "Have mercy on us O Lord, thou son of David." When he was in the house, the blind men came to him; and Jesus said to them, "Believe ye that I am able to do this?" They said to him, "Yea, Lord." Then he touched their eyes while he was saying, "According to your faith be it unto you." Their eyes were opened. Jesus then instructed them, "See that no man know it." But as they left, they told about him in all that country.

They were on their way out when a man was brought to him who could not speak and was possessed with a devil. When the devil was cast out, the dumb man spoke. The crowds were amazed and said, "It was never so seen in Israel." Then the Pharisees said, "He casteth out devils through the prince of devils."

# THE YEAR
# OF OPPOSITION

✠ *The Third Year of Christ's Ministry*

*The Twelve
Apostles Sent
Forth*

Jesus went to all the cities and towns, teaching in their synagogues, preaching the good news of the kingdom, and healing every sickness and disease among the people. The sight of the multitudes moved him to compassion because they were physically weak and as sheep that had no shepherd. At this time he said to his disciples, "The harvest truly is plenteous, but the labourers are few; pray ye therefore the Lord of the harvest, that he will send forth labourers into his harvest." Then he called to him his twelve disciples and gave them power to cast out unclean spirits and to heal all kinds of sickness and disease.

The names of the twelve apostles are: first, Simon, who is called Peter, and Andrew his brother, James, the son of Zebedee, and John his brother, Philip and Bartholomew, Thomas and Matthew the publican, James, the son of Alphaeus, and Lebbaeus, whose surname was Thaddaeus, Simon the Canaanite, and Judas Iscariot, who also betrayed him. Jesus sent forth these twelve, commanding them, "Go not into the way of the Gentiles, and into any city of the Samaritans enter ye not: but go rather to the lost sheep of the house of Israel. And as ye go, preach, saying, The kingdom of heaven is at hand. Heal the sick, cleanse the lepers, raise the dead, cast out devils: freely ye have received, freely give. Provide neither gold, nor silver, nor brass in your purses, nor scrip for your journey, neither two coats, neither shoes, nor yet staves: for the workman is worthy of his meat. And into whatsoever city or town ye shall enter, inquire who in it is worthy; and there abide till ye go thence. And when ye come into an house, salute it. And if the house be worthy, let your peace come upon it: but if it be not worthy, let your peace return to you. And whosoever shall not receive you, nor hear your words, when ye depart out of that house or city, shake off the dust of your feet. Verily I say unto you, it shall be more tolerable for the land of Sodom and Gomorrha in the day of judgment, than for that city.

"Behold, I send you forth as sheep in the midst of wolves: be ye therefore wise as serpents, and harmless as doves. But beware of men: for they will deliver you up to the councils, and they will scourge you in their synagogues; and ye shall be brought before governors and kings for my sake, for a testimony against them and the Gentiles. But when they deliver you up, take no thought how or what ye shall speak: for it shall be given you in that same hour what ye shall speak. For it is not ye that speak, but the Spirit of your Father which speaketh in you. And the brother shall deliver up the brother to death, and the father the child: and the children shall rise up against their parents, and cause them to be put to death. And ye shall be hated of all men for my name's sake: but he that endureth to the end shall be saved. But when they persecute you in this city, flee ye into another: for verily I say unto you, Ye shall not have gone over the cities of Israel, till the Son of man be come.

"The disciple is not above his master, nor the servant above his lord. It is enough for the disciple that he be as his master, and the servant as his lord. If they have called the master of the house Beelzebub, how much more shall

61

they call them of his household? Fear them not therefore: for there is nothing covered, that shall not be revealed; and hid, that shall not be known. What I tell you in darkness, that speak ye in light: and what ye hear in the ear, that preach ye upon the house tops. And fear not them which kill the body, but are not able to kill the soul: but rather fear him which is able to destroy both soul and body in hell. Are not two sparrows sold for a farthing? and one of them shall not fall on the ground without your Father? But the very hairs of your head are all numbered. Fear ye not therefore, ye are of more value than many sparrows. Whosoever therefore shall confess me before men, him will I confess also before my Father which is in heaven. But whosoever shall deny me before men, him will I also deny before my Father which is in heaven.

"I am come to send fire on the earth; and what will I, if it be already kindled? But I have a baptism to be baptized with; and how am I straitened till it be accomplished!

"Think not that I am come to send peace on earth: I came not to send peace, but a sword. For I am come to set a man at variance against his father, and the daughter against her mother, and the daughter in law against her mother in law. And a man's foes shall be they of his own household. He that loveth father or mother more than me is not worthy of me: and he that loveth son or daughter more than me is not worthy of me. And he that taketh not his cross, and followeth after me, is not worthy of me. He that findeth his life shall lose it: and he that loseth his life for my sake shall find it.

"He that receiveth you receiveth me, and he that receiveth me receiveth him that sent me. He that receiveth a prophet in the name of a prophet shall receive a prophet's reward; and he that receiveth a righteous man in the name of a righteous man shall receive a righteous man's reward. And whosoever shall give to drink unto one of

hese little ones a cup of cold water only in the name of
a disciple, verily I say unto you, he shall in no wise lose
his reward."

When Jesus had finished with his commands to his
twelve disciples, he went out to teach and to preach and
to heal throughout the country.

At this time Herod heard the reports concerning Jesus and said to his servants, "This is John the
Baptist; he is risen from the dead; and therefore mighty
works do shew forth themselves in him." Others said
that it is Elijah; and others said it is a prophet, or a person
like one of the prophets. But Herod insisted, "It is John,
whom I beheaded: he is risen from the dead."

*Beheading of
John the Bap-
tist*

For Herod himself had sent and arrested John and put
him in prison to please Herodias, his brother Philip's
wife, whom he had married. John had said to Herod, "It
is not lawful for thee to have thy brother's wife." Therefore Herodias was angry at him and would have killed
him, but she could not because Herod was afraid of John,
knowing he was a just and holy man, so he kept him in
jail. He was glad to hear what John had to say, though
he did not understand all that he said.

A convenient day for Herodias came when on his
birthday, Herod gave a supper for his officers and large
landholders of Galilee. When the daughter of Herodias
came in and danced, it so pleased Herod and his guests
that he said to the girl, "Ask of me whatsoever thou wilt,
and I will give it thee." He swore to her, "Whatsoever
thou shalt ask of me, I will give it thee, unto the half of
my kingdom." She went out and said to her mother,
"What shall I ask?" She replied, "The head of John the
Baptist." She hurried to the king and said, "I will that
thou give me by and by in a charger the head of John
the Baptist." The king was extremely sorry, yet for the
sake of his word, and because of his guests who had heard
him promise, he would not reject her. Immediately the
king sent an executioner with orders that his head be

63

brought. He went and beheaded him in prison, brought his head on a platter and gave it to the girl. The girl gave it to her mother. When his disciples heard of it, they came and claimed his body and laid it in a tomb.

*Feeding of the Five Thousand*

Later on Jesus went to the other side of the sea of Galilee, which is also known as the sea of Tiberias, and a large crowd followed him because they saw his miracles of healing the sick. Jesus went up on a mountainside and sat down there with his disciples. This was near the time of the Passover, a Jewish feast.

When Jesus looked up and saw a great crowd coming toward him, he said to Philip, "Whence shall we buy bread, that these may eat?" He said this to test him, for he himself knew what he would do. Philip answered, "Two hundred pennyworth of bread is not sufficient for them, that every one of them may take a little." One of his disciples, Andrew, Simon Peter's brother, said to him, "There is a lad here, which hath five barley loaves, and two small fishes: but what are they among so many?"

Jesus said, "Make the men sit down." This was a large, grassy place. There were about five thousand men, and they sat down. Jesus took the loaves, and when he had given thanks, he distributed it to the disciples, and the disciples to those sitting down. They did the same with the fishes and gave the people all they would take. When all had eaten all they wanted, he said to his disciples, "Gather up the fragments that remain, that nothing be lost." They gathered twelve baskets full of what was left over after the people had eaten.

When these men had seen the miracles Jesus did, they said, "This is of a truth that prophet that should come into the world." When Jesus saw that they would take him by force to make him a king, he went again on the mountain by himself to pray.

*Jesus Walking on the Sea*

As the night came, his disciples went down to the coast, got into a ship and started across the sea toward Capernaum. It had now become dark and Jesus had not yet come to them. The ship was now out on the sea, being tossed by waves and the wind was against them. Between three and six o'clock in the morning Jesus went to them, walking on the sea. When the disciples saw him walking on the sea, they were so disturbed that they cried out, "It is a spirit!"; and they were very afraid. Immediately Jesus spoke to them, saying, "Be of good cheer: it is I; be not afraid." Peter answered him, "Lord, if it be thou, bid me come unto thee on the water." He said, "Come." When Peter got over the side of the ship, he walked on the water toward Jesus. But when he saw the high wind, he was afraid, and beginning to sink, cried out, "Lord, save me." Then Jesus stretched out his hand, caught him, and said to him, "O thou of little faith, wherefore didst thou doubt?" When they got into the ship, the wind ceased. Those in the ship came and knelt before him and said, "Of a truth thou art the Son of God."

When they had crossed the sea, they came to the land of Gennesaret. When the people there learned of him, they sent around throughout the country and brought to him all that were sick. They begged him to let them touch the hem of his cloak, and all that touched were made completely well.

The next day when the people which were *The Bread of* left on the other side of the sea saw there was no other *Life* boat except the ones the disciples had taken, and knowing that Jesus had not gone with the disciples but saw that he was not there, they got into some boats which had come over from Tiberias and came to Capernaum to look for Jesus.

When they found him on the other side of the sea, they said to him, "Rabbi, whence camest thou hither?" Jesus answered them, "Verily, verily, I say unto you, Ye seek me, not because ye saw the miracles, but because ye did eat of the loaves, and were filled. Labour not for the meat which perisheth, but for that meat which endureth unto everlasting life, which the Son of man shall give unto

you: for him hath God the Father sealed." Then they
said to him, "What shall we do, that we might work the
works of God?" Jesus answered, "This is the work of
God, that ye believe on him whom he hath sent." Therefore they said to him, "What sign shewest thou then, that
we may see, and believe thee? what dost thou work? Our
fathers did eat manna in the desert; as it is written, He
gave them bread from heaven to eat." Then Jesus said
to them, "Verily, verily, I say unto you, Moses gave you
not that bread from heaven; but my Father giveth you
the true bread from heaven. For the bread of God is he
which cometh down from heaven, and giveth life unto
the world." Then they said to him, "Lord, evermore give
us this bread."

And Jesus said to them, "I am the bread of life: he
that cometh to me shall never hunger; and he that believeth on me shall never thirst. But I said unto you that
ye also have seen me, and believe not. All that the Father
giveth me shall come to me: and him that cometh to me
I will in no wise cast out. For I came down from heaven,
not to do mine own will, but the will of him that sent
me. And this is the Father's will which hath sent me, that
of all which he hath given me I should lose nothing, but
should raise it up again at the last day. And this is the
will of him that sent me, that every one which seeth the
Son, and believeth on him, may have everlasting life: and
I will raise him up at the last day."

The Jews then began grumbling at him, because he
said, "I am the bread which came down from heaven."
They said, "Is not this Jesus, the son of Joseph, whose
father and mother we know? how is it then that he saith,
I came down from heaven?"

Therefore Jesus answered them, "Murmur not among
yourselves. No man can come to me, except the Father
which hath sent me draw him: and I will raise him up
at the last day. It is written in the prophets, And they
shall be all taught of God. Every man therefore that hath

heard, and hath learned of the Father, cometh unto me. Not that any man hath seen the Father, save he which is of God, he hath seen the Father. Verily, verily, I say unto you, he that believeth on me hath everlasting life. I am that bread of life. Your fathers did eat manna in the wilderness, and are dead. This is the bread which cometh down from heaven, that a man may eat thereof, and not die. I am the living bread which came down from heaven: if any man eat of this bread, he shall live for ever: and the bread that I will give is my flesh, which I will give for the life of the world."

The Jews argued among themselves, saying, "How can this man give us his flesh to eat?" Then Jesus said to them, "Verily, verily, I say unto you, Except ye eat the flesh of the Son of man, and drink his blood, ye have no life in you. Whoso eateth my flesh, and drinketh my blood, hath eternal life; and I will raise him up at the last day. For my flesh is meat indeed, and my blood is drink indeed. He that eateth my flesh, and drinketh my blood, dwelleth in me, and I in him. As the living Father hath sent me, and I live by the Father: so he that eateth me, even he shall live by me. This is that bread which came down from heaven: not as your fathers did eat manna, and are dead: he that eateth of this bread shall live for ever."

He said these things in the synagogue as he taught in Capernaum. When they heard this, many of his disciples said, "This is an hard saying; who can bear it?" When Jesus learned that his disciples grumbled at what he had said, he told them, "Doth this offend you? What and if ye shall see the Son of man ascend up where he was before? It is the spirit that quickeneth; the flesh profiteth nothing: the words that I speak unto you, they are spirit, and they are life. But there are some of you that believe not." For Jesus knew from the beginning the ones who would not believe and who would betray him. Thus he said, "Therefore said I unto you, that no man can come unto me, except it were given unto him of my Father."

From that time many of his disciples turned back and did not walk with him again. Then Jesus said to the twelve, "Will ye also go away?" Simon Peter answered him, "Lord, to whom shall we go? thou hast the words of eternal life. And we believe and are sure that thou art that Christ, the Son of the living God." Jesus answered them, "Have not I chosen you twelve, and one of you is a devil?" He spoke of Judas Iscariot, the son of Simon; for it was he that would betray him, being one of the twelve.

*Christ Re-*
*proved the*
*Pharisees*

Some scribes and Pharisees from Jerusalem came to him. When they saw some of his disciples eat bread with unwashed hands, they criticized them. The Pharisees and all the Jews held to the tradition of the elders which was never to eat until they had washed their hands. Also, they took great care to wash cups, pots and other vessels, even tables.

Then the Pharisees and scribes asked him, "Why walk not thy disciples according to the tradition of the elders, but eat bread with unwashen hands?" He replied to them, "Well hath Esaias prophesied of you hypocrites, as it is written,

This people honoureth me with their lips,
But their heart is far from me.
Howbeit in vain do they worship me,
Teaching for doctrines the commandments of men.

For laying aside the commandment of God, ye hold the tradition of men, as the washing of pots and cups: and many other such like things ye do." And he said to them, "Full well ye reject the commandment of God, that ye may keep your own tradition. For Moses said, Honour thy father and thy mother; and, whoso curseth father or mother, let him die the death: but ye say, If a man shall say to his father or mother, That wherewith thou mightest have been profited by me is Corban, that is to say, Given to God, ye no longer suffer him to do ought for his father or his mother; making the word of God of none effect through your tradition, which ye have delivered: and many such like things do ye."

Then his disciples came and said to him, "Knowest thou that the Pharisees were offended, after they heard this saying?" But he answered, "Every plant, which my heavenly Father hath not planted, shall be rooted up. Let them alone: they be blind leaders of the blind. And if the blind lead the blind, both shall fall into the ditch."

When he had entered the house to get away from the people, his disciples asked him about the parable. He said to them, "Are ye so without understanding also? Do ye not perceive, that whatsoever thing from without entereth into the man, it cannot defile him; because it entereth not into his heart, but into the belly, and goeth out into the draught, purging all meats?" And he said, "That which cometh out of the man, that defileth the man. For from within, out of the heart of men, proceed evil thoughts, adulteries, fornications, murders, thefts, covetousness, wickedness, deceit, lasciviousness, an evil eye, blasphemy, pride, foolishness: all these evil things come from within, and defile the man."

Then Jesus left and went to the coasts of Tyre and Sidon. He went into a house and did not want anyone to know it, but he could not be hidden. A woman of Canaan from that area cried to him, "Have mercy on me, O Lord, thou Son of David: my daughter is grievously vexed with a devil." He did not reply to her. And his disciples came and urged him, "Send her away; for she crieth after us." But he answered, "I am not sent but unto the lost sheep of the house of Israel." Then she came and knelt before him, saying, "Lord, help me!" But he answered, "It is not meet to take the children's bread, and to cast it to dogs." And she said, "Truth, Lord: yet the dogs eat of the crumbs which fall from their masters' table." Then Jesus answered, "O woman, great is thy faith: be it unto thee even as thou wilt," and her daughter

*A Woman's Daughter Healed*

was made well from that very hour. And when she reached her house, she found the devil gone out, and her daughter was lying on the bed.

**Deaf and Dumb Man Healed**

Leaving the coast of Tyre and Sidon, he came through the midst of the coasts of Decapolis to the sea of Galilee, went up on a mountain side and sat down there. Great multitudes came to him, bringing with them those that were lame, blind, dumb, crippled, and many others. They flung them down at Jesus' feet and he healed them. The people were amazed when they saw the dumb speak, the crippled healed, the lame walk and the blind see. They praised the God of Israel. They brought to him one that was deaf and had an impediment in his speech, and they begged him to put his hand upon him. He took him a short distance from the multitude, put his fingers into his ears, spat, and touched his tongue. Looking up to heaven, he sighed and said to him, "Ephphatha," which means, "Be opened." Right then his ears were opened, the string of his tongue was loosed, and he spoke plainly. He charged them that they should tell no man. But the more he charged them, the more they told it, and they were astonished beyond measure. They said, "He hath done all things well: he maketh both the deaf to hear, and the dumb to speak."

**The Feeding of the Four Thousand**

At this time, because the large multitude had nothing to eat, Jesus called his disciples to him and said, "I have compassion on the multitude, because they have now been with me three days, and have nothing to eat: and if I send them away fasting to their own houses, they will faint by the way: for divers of them came from far." His disciples answered him, "From whence can a man satisfy these men with bread here in the wilderness?" He asked them, "How many loaves have ye?" They said, "Seven." He commanded the people to sit down on the ground. He took the seven loaves, gave thanks, and broke, and gave to his disciples to offer the people. They did so. They had a few small fishes. These he blessed and com-

manded they be set before the people, also. They ate and
were filled. Then they took up seven baskets of the
broken meat that was left. There were about four thousand who ate.

He sent the multitude away and took a ship to the
coasts of Magadan.

The Pharisees and also the Sadducees came *Pharisees Seek*
and temptingly asked him to show them a sign from *a Sign*
heaven. He said to them, "When it is evening, ye say,
it will be fair weather: for the sky is red. And in the morning, It will be foul weather to day: for the sky is red
and lowering. O ye hypocrites, ye can discern the face
of the sky; but can ye not discern the signs of the times?
A wicked and adulterous generation seeketh after a sign;
and there shall no sign be given unto it, but the sign of
the prophet Jonas." And he left them, and departed.

When his disciples got to the other side, they had for-
gotten to take bread with them and had not more than
one loaf on the ship with them. Jesus said to them, "Take
heed and beware of the leaven of the Pharisees and of the
Sadducees." They discussed it among themselves and said,
"It is because we have taken no bread." When Jesus realized what they were saying, he told them, "O ye of
little faith, why reason ye among yourselves, because ye
have brought no bread? Do ye not yet understand,
neither remember the five loaves of the five thousand, and
how many baskets ye took up? neither the seven loaves
of the four thousand, and how many baskets ye took up?
How is it that ye do not understand that I spake it not
to you concerning bread, that ye should beware of the
leaven of the Pharisees and of the Sadducees?" Then
they understood that he did not mean the leaven of bread
but was referring to the doctrine of the Pharisees and
of the Sadducees.

He came to Bethsaida and they brought a blind *The Blind Man*
man to him and asked him to touch him. He took the *Near Bethsaida*
blind man by the hand and led him outside the town.

When he had spit on his eyes and put his hands upon him, he asked him if he saw anything. He looked up and said, "I see men as trees, walking." After that, he put his hands on his eyes again and made him look up. He then was restored and saw every man clearly. He sent him to his house and said to him, "Neither go into the town, nor tell it to any in the town."

*Peter's Con-*
*fession*

When Jesus came to the coasts of Caesarea Philippi, he asked his disciples, "Whom do men say that I the Son of man am?" They said, "Some say that thou art John the Baptist: some, Elias; and others, Jeremias, or one of the prophets." He said to them, "But whom say ye that I am?" Simon Peter answered, "Thou art the Christ, the Son of the living God!" Jesus said unto him, "Blessed art thou, Simon Bar-jona: for flesh and blood hath not revealed it unto thee, but my Father which is in heaven. And I say also unto thee, That thou art Peter, and upon this rock I will build my church; and the gates of hell shall not prevail against it. And I will give unto thee the keys of the kingdom of heaven: and whatsoever thou shalt bind on earth shall be bound in heaven: and whatsoever thou shalt loose on earth shall be loosed in heaven." Then he commanded his disciples that they should not tell anyone that he was Jesus the Christ.

*Death and*
*Resurrection*
*Foretold*

From that time on Jesus began to explain to his disciples how it was necessary for him to go to Jerusalem, suffer many things from the elders, chief priests and scribes, be killed, and be raised on the third day. Peter took hold of him and began to rebuke him: "Be it far from thee, Lord: this shall not be unto thee." He turned and said to Peter, "Get thee behind me, Satan: thou art an offence unto me: for thou savourest not the things that be of God, but those that be of men."

Then Jesus said to his disciples, "If any man will come after me, let him deny himself, and take up his cross, and follow me. For whosoever will save his life shall lose it: and whosoever will lose his life for my sake shall find it.

For what is a man profited, if he shall gain the whole world, and lose his own soul? or what shall a man give in exchange for his soul? For the Son of man shall come in the glory of his Father with the angels; and then he shall reward every man according to his works. Verily I say unto you, There be some standing here, which shall not taste of death, till they see the Son of man coming in his kingdom."

About eight days after this, he took Peter, John and James and went up on a high mountain to pray. As he prayed the appearance of his face was changed and his clothes were white and glistening. Suddenly two men were talking with him, who were Moses and Elias, robed in heavenly glory, and they spoke of his departure which he would accomplish in Jerusalem. Peter and those with him were soundly asleep, and when they were awake, they saw his glory and the two men that stood with him. As they were walking away from him, Peter said to Jesus, "Master, it is good for us to be here: and let us make three tabernacles; one for thee, and one for Moses, and one for Elias," but he spoke without knowing what he was saying. While he spoke, a cloud came and covered them, and they were afraid as they entered into the cloud. A voice came out of the cloud, saying, "This is my beloved son: hear him." When the voice was gone, Jesus was there alone.

*The Trans-
figuration*

As they came down from the mountain, he told them that they should not tell any person what they had seen, until the Son of man was risen from the dead. They did as they were told, at the same time questioning among themselves what the rising from the dead meant. They asked him, "Why say the scribes that Elias must come first?" He told them, "Elias verily cometh first, and restoreth all things; and how it is written of the Son of man, that he must suffer many things, and be set at nought. But I say unto you, That Elias is indeed come, and they have done unto him whatsoever they listed, as it is written of him."

*The Demoniac
Son*

When he got to his disciples, he saw a large crowd gathered around them and the scribes were questioning with them. When the people saw him, they were amazed and ran to greet him. He asked the scribes, "What question ye with them?" One of the crowd answered, "Master, I have brought unto thee my son, mine only son, which hath a dumb spirit; and wheresoever he taketh him, he teareth him: and he foameth, and gnasheth with his teeth, and pineth away: and I spake to thy disciples that they should cast him out; and they could not." He answereth him, "O faithless generation, how long shall I be with you? how long shall I suffer you? bring him unto me."

And they brought the boy to him, and when the spirit saw him, immediately it threw the boy into convulsions and he fell on the ground, rolling about and foaming at the mouth. He asked the father, "How long is it ago since this came unto him?" He said, "Of a child. And ofttimes it hath cast him into the fire, and into the waters, to destroy him: but if thou canst do any thing, have compassion on us, and help us." Jesus said to him, "If thou canst believe, all things are possible to him that believeth." Then the father cried out and said with tears in his eyes, "Lord, I believe; help thou mine unbelief!"

When Jesus saw that the crowd was rapidly closing in, he rebuked the foul spirit, saying to him, "Thou dumb and deaf spirit, I charge thee, come out of him, and enter no more into him." The spirit made a loud outcry, shook the boy violently, and came out of him. He lay so still that many said, "He is dead." But Jesus took him by the hand, lifted him up and he stood.

When he got into the house, his disciples asked him privately, "Why could not we cast him out?" He said to them, "This kind can come forth by nothing, but by prayer and fasting."

*He Foretells
His Passion*

They left there and passed through Galilee, and he did not want any man to know it. He explained to his disciples, "The Son of man is delivered into the hands of men, and they shall kill him; and after that he is killed, he shall rise the third day." They did not understand what he had said and were afraid to ask him.

When they arrived in Capernaum, the collectors of the temple tax came to Peter and asked, "Doth not your master pay tribute?" He said, "Yes." When he got into the house, Jesus prevented him from speaking by asking, "What thinkest thou, Simon? of whom do the kings of the earth take custom or tribute? of their own children, or of strangers?" Peter replied, "Of strangers." Jesus said to him, "Then are the children free. Notwithstanding, lest we should offend them, go thou to the sea, and cast an hook, and take up the fish that first cometh up; and when thou hast opened his mouth, thou shalt find a piece of money: that take, and give unto them for me and thee."

*Money in the Fish's Mouth*

While in the house in Capernaum, he asked the disciples, "What was it that ye disputed among yourselves by the way?" But they did not reply because they had been arguing about who should be the greatest. He sat down, called the twelve around him, and said, "If any man desire to be first, the same shall be last of all, and servant of all." Jesus called a little child to him, and set him in the middle of them, and said, "Verily I say unto you, Except ye be converted; and become as little children, ye shall not enter into the kingdom of heaven. Whosoever therefore shall humble himself as this little child, the same is greatest in the kingdom of heaven. And whoso shall receive one such little child in my name receiveth me; and whosoever shall receive me receiveth him that sent me."

*Jesus Teaches Humility and Forgiveness*

John answered him, "Master, we saw one casting out devils in thy name, and he followeth not us: and we forbad him, because he followeth not us." Jesus said, "Forbid him not: for there is no man which shall do a miracle in my name, that can lightly speak evil of me. For he that is not against us is on our part. For whosoever shall give you a cup of water to drink in my name,

because ye belong to Christ, verily I say unto you, he
shall not lose his reward. And whosoever shall offend one
of these little ones that believe in me, it is better for him
that a millstone were hanged about his neck, and he were
cast into the sea. Woe unto the world because of offences!
for it must needs be that offences come; but woe to that
man by whom the offence cometh! Take heed that ye
despise not one of these little ones; for I say unto you,
That in heaven their angels do always behold the face of
my Father which is in heaven. Moreover if thy brother
shall trespass against thee, go and tell him his fault between thee and him alone: if he shall hear thee, thou hast
gained thy brother. But if he will not hear thee, then take
with thee one or two more, that in the mouth of two or
three witnesses every word may be established. And if
he shall neglect to hear them, tell it unto the church:
but if he neglect to hear the church, let him be unto thee
as an heathen man and a publican. Verily I say unto you,
whatsoever ye shall bind on earth shall be bound in
heaven: and whatsoever ye shall loose on earth shall be
loosed in heaven. Again I say unto you, That if two of
you shall agree on earth as touching any thing that they
shall ask, it shall be done for them of my Father which
is in heaven. For where two or three are gathered together
in my name, there am I in the midst of them."

Then Peter came to him, and said, "Lord, how oft
shall my brother sin against me, and I forgive him? till
seven times?" Jesus said to him, "I say not unto thee,
Until seven times: but, Until seventy times seven. Therefore is the kingdom of heaven likened unto a certain
king, which would take account of his servants. And
when he had begun to reckon, one was brought unto
him, which owed him ten thousand talents. But forasmuch
as he had not to pay, his lord commanded him to be
sold, and his wife, and children, and all that he had, and
payment to be made. The servant therefore fell down, and
worshipped him, saying, Lord, have patience with me,

76 |

and I will pay thee all. Then the lord of that servant was moved with compassion, and loosed him, and forgave him the debt. But the same servant went out, and found one of his fellow servants, which owed him an hundred pence: and he laid hands on him and took him by the throat, saying, Pay me that thou owest. And his fellow servant fell down at his feet, and besought him, saying, Have patience with me, and I will pay thee all. And he would not: but went and cast him into prison, till he should pay the debt. So when his fellow servants saw what was done, they were very sorry, and came and told unto their lord all that was done. Then his lord, after that he had called him, said unto him, O thou wicked servant, I forgave thee all that debt, because thou desiredst me: shouldest not thou also have had compassion on thy fellow servant, even as I had pity on thee? And his lord was wroth, and delivered him to the tormentors, till he should pay all that was due unto him. So likewise shall my heavenly Father do also unto you, if ye from your hearts forgive not every one his brother his trespasses."

After this Jesus went about in Galilee. He would not go to Judea because the Jews were seeking an opportunity to kill him. *Jesus at the Feast of Tabernacles*

It was time for the Jews' Feast of Tabernacles. His brothers said to him, "Depart hence, and go into Judaea, that thy disciples also may see the works that thou doest. For there is no man that doeth any thing in secret, and he himself seeketh to be known openly. If thou do these things, shew thyself to the world." For his brothers did not believe in him, either.

Jesus replied to them, "My time is not yet come: but your time is alway ready. The world cannot hate you; but me it hateth, because I testify of it, that the works thereof are evil. Go ye up unto this feast: I go not up yet unto this feast; for my time is not yet full come." When Jesus had spoken these words to them, he remained in Galilee.

But after his brothers were gone to the feast, he went also, not openly, however, but in secret. The Jews looked for him at the feast and asked, "Where is he?" There was much discussion among the people about him; for some said, "He is a good man": others said, "Nay; but he deceiveth the people." However, no one spoke publicly about him because of their fear of the Jews.

About midway of the feast Jesus went into the temple and taught. The Jews marveled, saying, "How knoweth this man letters, having never learned?" Jesus answered them, "My doctrine is not mine, but his that sent me. If any man will do his will, he shall know of the doctrine, whether it be of God, or whether I speak of myself. He that speaketh of himself seeketh his own glory: but he that seeketh his glory that sent him, the same is true, and no unrighteousness is in him. Did not Moses give you the law, and yet none of you keepeth the law? Why go ye about to kill me?" The people replied, "Thou hast a devil: who goeth about to kill thee?" Jesus said to them, "I have done one work, and ye all marvel. Moses therefore gave unto you circumcision; (not because it is of Moses, but of the fathers;) and ye on the sabbath day circumcise a man. If a man on the sabbath day receive circumcision, that the law of Moses should not be broken; are ye angry at me, because I have made a man every whit whole on the sabbath day? Judge not according to the appearance, but judge righteous judgment."

Then some of them of Jerusalem said, "Is not this he, whom they seek to kill? But, lo, he speaketh boldly, and they say nothing unto him. Do the rulers know indeed that this is the very Christ? Howbeit we know this man whence he is: but when Christ cometh, no man knoweth whence he is."

Then Jesus spoke loudly, "Ye both know me, and ye know whence I am: and I am not come of myself, but he that sent me is true, whom ye know not. But I know him: for I am from him, and he hath sent me."

They made an effort to take him but no man put hands on him because his hour had not yet come.

Many of the people believed on him, and said, "When Christ cometh, will he do more miracles than these which this man hath done? The Pharisees heard that the people murmured such things concerning him, and the Pharisees and the chief priests sent officers to take him. Then Jesus said to them, "Yet a little while I am with you, and then I go unto him that sent me. Ye shall seek me, and shall not find me: and where I am, thither ye cannot come." Then said the Jews among themselves, "Whither will he go, that we shall not find him? will he go unto the dispersed among the Gentiles, and teach the Gentiles? What manner of saying is this that he said, Ye shall seek me, and shall not find me: and where I am, thither ye cannot come"?

On the last day of the feast, which was the climax, Jesus stood up and spoke loudly, "If any man thirst, let him come unto me, and drink. He that believeth on me, as the scripture hath said, out of his belly shall flow rivers of living water." But he was speaking of the Spirit which believers in him would receive but which had not yet come because Jesus had not yet been glorified.

When they had heard what he said, many of the people said, "Of a truth this is the prophet." Others said, "This is the Christ." But some said, "Shall Christ come out of Galilee? Hath not the scripture said, That Christ cometh of the seed of David, and out of the town of Bethlehem, where David was?" So the people disputed among themselves because of him. Some of them would like to have taken him but no one laid hands on him.

The police of the temple came to the chief priests and Pharisees and were asked, "Why have ye not brought him?" The police answered, "Never man spake like this man." Then the Pharisees answered, "Are ye also deceived? Have any of the rulers or of the Pharisees believed on him? But this people who knoweth not the law are cursed." Nicodemus, the one who came by night and was one of them, said, "Doth our law judge any man, before it hear him, and knoweth what he doeth?" They said to him, "Art thou also of Galilee? Search, and look: for out of Galilee ariseth no prophet."

All the people went home but Jesus went to the Mount of Olives.

Early the next morning he again came to the temple and the people gathered around him. He sat down and taught them.

*The Woman Taken in Adultery*

The scribes and Pharisees brought to him a woman who had been caught in the act of adultery. When they sat her in the center, they said to him, "Master, this woman was taken in adultery, in the very act. Now Moses in the law commanded us, that such should be stoned: but what sayest thou?" They said this to test him so they might have an accusation against him. Jesus stooped down and wrote on the ground with his finger, as though he had not heard them. When they continued to ask him, he stood up and said to them, "He that is without sin among you, let him first cast a stone at her." Again he stooped down and wrote on the ground.

Those who heard it, being convicted by their own conscience, went out one by one, beginning with the oldest until all had gone. Jesus was left alone with the woman standing there.

When Jesus stood up and saw none but the woman, he said to her, "Woman, where are those thine accusers? hath no man condemned thee?" She said, "No man, Lord." Jesus said to her, "Neither do I condemn thee: go, and sin no more."

*The Light of the World*

Jesus spoke to the people again and said, "I am the light of the world: he that followeth me shall not walk in darkness, but shall have the light of life."

Therefore, the Pharisees said to him, "Thou bearest record of thyself; thy record is not true." Jesus replied to them, "Though I bear record of myself, yet my record is true: for I know whence I came, and whither I go: but ye cannot tell whence I come, and whither I go. Ye judge after the flesh; I judge no man. And yet if I judge, my judgment is true: for I am not alone, but I and the Father that sent me. It is also written in your law, that the testimony of two men is true. I am one that bear witness of myself, and the Father that sent me beareth witness of me."

Then they said to him, "Where is thy Father?" Jesus answered, "Ye neither know me, nor my Father: if ye had known me, ye should have known my Father also."

Jesus spoke these words in the treasury as he taught in the temple. No man put his hands on him because his hour had not yet come.

Jesus spoke again and said to them, "I go my way, and ye shall seek me, and shall die in your sins: whither I go, ye cannot come." Then the Jews said, "Will he kill himself, because he saith, Whither I go, ye cannot come"? He said to them, "Ye are from beneath; I am from above: ye are of this world; I am not of this world. I said therefore unto you, that ye shall die in your sins: for if ye believe not that I am he, ye shall die in your sins."

Then they said to him, "Who art thou?" Jesus replied, "Even the same that I said unto you from the beginning. I have many things to say and to judge of you: but he that sent me is true; and I speak to the world those things which I have heard of him." They did not understand that he was speaking to them of the Father.

Then Jesus said to them, "When ye have lifted up the Son of man, then shall ye know that I am he, and that I do nothing of myself; but as my Father hath taught me, I speak these things. And he that sent me is with me: the Father hath not left me alone; for I do always those things that please him."

As he spoke these words, many believed in him. Then Jesus said to the Jews who believed in him, "If ye continue in my word, then are ye my disciples indeed; and ye shall know the truth, and the truth shall make you free." They answered him, "We be Abraham's seed, and were never in bondage to any man: how sayest thou, Ye shall be made free"?

Jesus answered them, "Verily, verily, I say unto you, Whosoever committeth sin is the servant of sin. And the servant abideth not in the house for ever: but the Son abideth ever. If the Son therefore shall make you free, ye shall be free indeed. I know that ye are Abraham's seed; but ye seek to kill me, because my word hath no place in you. I speak that which I have seen with my Father: and ye do that which ye have seen with your father." They replied to him, "Abraham is our Father." Jesus said to them, "If ye were Abraham's children, ye would do the works of Abraham. But now ye seek to kill me, a man that hath told you the truth, which I have heard of God: this did not Abraham. Ye do the deeds of your father."

Then they said to him, "We be not born of fornication; we have one Father, even God." Jesus answered, "If God were your Father, ye would love me: for I proceeded forth and came from God; neither came I of myself, but he sent me. Why do ye not understand my speech? Even because you cannot hear my word. Ye are of your father, the devil, and the lusts of your father ye will do. He was a murderer from the beginning, and abode not in the truth, because there is no truth in him. When he speaketh a lie, he speaketh of his own: for he is a liar, and the father of it. And because I tell you the truth, ye believe me not. Which of you convinceth me of sin? And if I say the truth, why do ye not believe me? He that is of God heareth God's words: ye therefore hear them not, because ye are not of God."

Then the Jews answered him, "Say we not well that thou art a Samaritan, and hast a devil?" Jesus answered, "I have not a devil; but I honour my Father, and ye do dishonour me. And I seek not mine own glory: there is

82 |

one that seeketh and judgeth. Verily, verily, I say unto you, If a man keep my saying, he shall never see death."

Then the Jews said to him, "Now we know that thou hast a devil. Abraham is dead, and the prophets; and thou sayest, if a man keep my saying, he shall never taste of death. Art thou greater than our father Abraham, which is dead? and the prophets are dead: whom makest thou thyself?"

Jesus answered, "If I honour myself, my honour is nothing: it is my Father that honoureth me; of whom ye say, that he is your God: yet ye have not known him; but I know him: and if I should say, I know him not, I shall be a liar like unto you: but I know him, and keep his saying. Your father Abraham rejoiced to see my day: and he saw it, and was glad." Then the Jews said to him, "Thou are not yet fifty years old, and hast thou seen Abraham?" Jesus said to them, "Verily, verily, I say unto you, Before Abraham was, I am."

Then they picked up stones to throw at him, but Jesus hid and went out of the temple, going through the middle of them.

It happened that when Jesus had completed these sayings, he left for Galilee and came to the coasts of Judea beyond Jordan. Great multitudes followed him and he healed them there. *James and John Reproved*

When the time neared that he was to be taken up to heaven, he steadfastly determined to go to Jerusalem and sent messengers on ahead. They went to a Samaritan village to get ready for him. The people in the village would not receive him because he seemed to be on the way to Jerusalem. When his disciples James and John saw this, they said, "Lord, wilt thou that we command fire to come down from heaven, and consume them, even as Elias did?" He turned around and rebuked them, and said, "Ye know not what manner of spirit ye are of. For the Son of man is not come to destroy men's lives, but to save them." They went to another village.

It happened that, as they walked along, a certain man said to him, "Lord, I will follow thee whithersoever thou goest." Jesus said to him, "Foxes have holes, and birds of the air have nests; but the Son of man hath not where to lay his head." He said to another, "Follow me." But he said, "Lord, suffer me first to go and bury my father." Jesus said to him, "Let the dead bury their dead: but go thou and preach the kingdom of God." Also another said, "Lord, I will follow thee; but let me first go bid them farewell, which are at home at my house." Jesus said to him, "No man, having put his hand to the plough, and looking back, is fit for the kingdom of God."

*Seventy Dis-*
*ciples Sent*
*Forth*

After this, Jesus appointed an additional seventy, and sent them two by two ahead of him to every city and place where he himself would come. He said to them, "The harvest truly is great, but the labourers are few: pray ye therefore the Lord of the harvest, that he would send forth labourers into his harvest. Go your ways: behold, I send you forth as lambs among wolves. Carry neither purse, nor scrip, nor shoes: and salute no man by the way. And into whatsoever house ye enter, first say, Peace be to this house. And if the son of peace be there, your peace shall rest upon it: if not, it shall turn to you again. And in the same house remain, eating and drinking such things as they give: for the labourer is worthy of his hire. Go not from house to house. And into whatsoever city ye enter, and they receive you, eat such things as are set before you: and heal the sick that are therein, and say unto them, The Kingdom of God is come nigh unto you. But into whatsoever city ye enter, and they receive you not, go your ways out into the streets of the same, and say, Even the very dust of your city, which cleaveth on us, we do wipe off against you: notwithstanding be ye sure of this, that the kingdom of God is come nigh unto you. But I say unto you, that it shall be more tolerable in that day for Sodom, than for that city. Woe unto thee, Chorazin! woe unto thee,

Bethsaida! For if the mighty works had been done in Tyre and Sidon, which have been done in you, they had a great while ago repented, sitting in sackcloth and ashes. But it shall be more tolerable for Tyre and Sidon at the judgment, than for you. And thou, Capernaum, which art exalted to heaven, shalt be thrust down to hell. He that heareth you heareth me; and he that despiseth you despiseth me; and he that despiseth me despiseth him that sent me."

The seventy returned with joy, saying, "Lord, even the devils are subject unto us through thy name." He said to them, "I beheld Satan as lightning fall from heaven. Behold, I give unto you power to tread on serpents and scorpions, and over all the power of the enemy: and nothing shall by any means hurt you. Notwithstanding in this rejoice not, that the spirits are subject unto you; but rather rejoice, because your names are written in heaven."

At this time Jesus rejoiced in spirit and said, "I thank thee, O Father, Lord of heaven and earth, that thou hast hid these things from the wise and prudent, and hast revealed them unto babes: even so, Father; for so it seemed good in thy sight. All things are delivered to me of my Father: and no man knoweth who the Son is, but the Father; and who the Father is, but the Son, and he to whom the Son will reveal him."

He turned him unto his disciples and said privately, "Blessed are the eyes which see the things that ye see: for I tell you, that many prophets and kings have desired to see those things which ye see, and have not seen them; and to hear those things which ye hear, and have not heard them."

A lawyer stood up and tested him, saying, *The Good* "Master, what shall I do to inherit eternal life?" He said *Samaritan* to him, "What is written in the law? how readest thou?" He answered, "Thou shalt love the Lord thy God with all thy heart, and with all thy soul, and with all thy

| 85

strength, and with all thy mind; and thy neighbour as thyself." He said to him, "Thou hast answered right: this do, and thou shalt live." But he, wanting to justify himself, said to Jesus, "And who is my neighbour?"

Jesus answered, "A certain man went down from Jerusalem to Jericho, and fell among thieves, which stripped him of his raiment, and wounded him, and departed, leaving him half dead. And by chance there came down a certain priest that way: and when he saw him, he passed by on the other side. And likewise a Levite, when he was at the place, came and looked on him, and passed by on the other side. But a certain Samaritan, as he journeyed, came where he was: and when he saw him, he had compassion on him, and went to him, and bound up his wounds, pouring in oil and wine, and set him on his own beast, and brought him to an inn, and took care of him. And on the morrow when he departed, he took out two pence, and gave them to the host, and said unto him, take care of him; and whatsoever thou spendest more, when I come again, I will repay thee. Which now of these three, thinkest thou, was neighbour unto him that fell among the thieves?" He said, "He that shewed mercy on him." Then said Jesus to him, "Go, and do thou likewise."

*Martha and Mary*

As they traveled along, he went into a village and a woman named Martha received him into her house. She had a sister named Mary, who sat at Jesus' feet and listened to him talk. Martha was burdened with preparing dinner and came to him and said, "Lord, dost thou not care that my sister hath left me to serve alone? bid her therefore that she help me." Jesus answered her, "Martha, Martha, thou are careful and troubled about many things: but one thing is needful: and Mary hath chosen that good part, which shall not be taken away from her."

*The Man Born Blind*

As Jesus passed by, he saw a man who had been blind from birth. His disciples asked him, "Master, who did sin, this man or his parents, that he was born

blind?" Jesus answered, "Neither hath this man sinned,
nor his parents: but that the works of God should be
made manifest in him. I must work the works of him
that sent me, while it is day: the night cometh, when
no man can work. As long as I am in the world, I am
the light of the world."

When he had finished speaking, he spat on the ground,
made clay of the spittle, and covered the blind man's eyes
with the clay. Then he said to him, "Go, wash in the
pool of Siloam."

He went and washed and came away seeing. The
neighbors and others who had known him who was
blind said, "Is not this he that sat and begged?" Some
said, "This is he"; and others said, "He is like him"; but
he said, "I am he." Therefore they said to him, "How
were thine eyes opened?" He answered, "A man that
is called Jesus made clay, and anointed mine eyes, and
said unto me, Go to the pool of Siloam, and wash: and
I went and washed, and I received sight." Then they said
to him, "Where is he?" He said, "I know not."

They brought to the Pharisees the man who before had
been blind. It was on the Sabbath day when Jesus made
the clay and opened his eyes. The Pharisees asked him
over again how he had received his sight. He said to
them, "He put clay upon mine eyes, and I washed, and
do see." Therefore some of the Pharisees said, "This man
is not of God, because he keepeth not the sabbath day."
Others said, "How can a man that is a sinner do such
miracles?" There was a division among them. They said
to the blind man again, "What sayest thou of him, that
he hath opened thine eyes?" He said, "He is a prophet."

But the Jews did not believe that the man had been
blind and received his sight until they talked to his
parents. They asked them, "Is this your son, who ye say
was born blind? how then doth he now see?" His parents
answered, "We know that this is our son, and that he
was born blind: but by what means he now seeth, we
know not; or who hath opened his eyes, we know not:

he is of age; ask him: he shall speak for himself." His parents said this because they were afraid of the Jews, because the Jews had already agreed that any who confessed that he was the Christ would be turned out of the synagogue. Therefore his parents said, "He is of age; ask him."

Again they called the man who had been blind and said to him, "Give God the praise: we know that this man is a sinner." He answered, "Whether he be a sinner or no, I know not: one thing I know, that, whereas I was blind, now I see." They said to him again, "What did he to thee? how opened he thine eyes?" He answered them, "I have told you already, and ye did not hear: wherefore would ye hear it again? will ye also be his disciples?"

Then they abused him, and said, "Thou art his disciples; but we are Moses' disciples. We know that God spake unto Moses: as for this fellow, we know not from whence he is." The man answered, "Why, herein is a marvellous thing, that ye know not from whence he is, and yet he hath opened mine eyes. Now we know that God heareth not sinners: but if any man be a worshipper of God, and doeth his will, him he heareth. Since the world began was it not heard that any man opened the eyes of one that was born blind. If this man were not of God, he could do nothing." They said to him, "Thou wast altogether born in sins, and dost thou teach us?" And they dismissed him from the synagogue.

Jesus heard that they had expelled the man. When he found him, he said, "Dost thou believe on the Son of man?" He answered, "Who is he, Lord, that I might believe on him?" Jesus said to him, "Thou hast both seen him, and it is he that talketh with thee," and he said, "Lord, I believe." And he knelt before him.

Jesus said, "For judgment I am come into this world, that they which see not might see: and that they which see might be made blind."

Some of the Pharisees who were with him and heard
what he said, said to him, "Are we blind also?" Jesus
said to them, "If ye were blind, ye should have no sin:
but now ye say, We see; therefore your sin remaineth.

"Verily, verily, I say unto you, He that entereth not
by the door into the sheepfold, but climbeth up some
other way, the same is a thief and a robber. But he that
entereth in by the door is the shepherd of the sheep.
To him the porter openeth; and the sheep hear his voice:
and he calleth his own sheep by name, and leadeth them
out. And when he putteth forth his own sheep, he goeth
before them, and the sheep follow him: for they know
his voice. And a stranger will they not follow, but will
flee from him: for they know not the voice of strangers."

Jesus spoke this parable to them but they did not
understand it.

Then Jesus spoke again, "Verily, verily, I say *The Good*
unto you, I am the door of the sheep. All that ever *Shepherd*
came before me are thieves and robbers: but the sheep
did not hear them. I am the door: by me if any man enter
in, he shall be saved, and shall go in and out, and find
pasture. The thief cometh not, but for to steal, and to
kill, and to destroy: I am come that they might have
life, and that they might have it more abundantly. I am
the good shepherd: the good shepherd giveth his life
for the sheep. But he that is a hireling, and not the
shepherd, whose own the sheep are not, seeth the wolf
coming, and leaveth the sheep, and fleeth: and the wolf
catcheth them, and scattereth the sheep. The hireling
fleeth, because he is an hireling, and careth not for the
sheep. I am the good shepherd, and know my sheep,
and am known of mine. As the Father knoweth me, even
so know I the Father: and I lay down my life for the
sheep. And other sheep I have, which are not of this
fold: them also I must bring, and they shall hear my
voice; and there shall be one fold, and one shepherd.
Therefore doth my Father love me, because I lay down

my life, that I might take it again. No man taketh it
from me, but I lay it down of myself. I have power to
lay it down, and I have power to take it again. This
commandment have I received of my Father."

Again the Jews were divided over these things which
Jesus had said. Many of them said, "He hath a devil, and
is mad; why hear ye him?" Others said, "These are not
the words of him that hath a devil. Can a devil open the
eyes of the blind?"

*The Feast of
the Dedication*
        The Feast of Dedication was at Jerusalem, and
it was during the winter. Jesus walked in the Temple in
Solomon's porch. The Jews gathered about him and
said, "How long dost thou make us to doubt? If thou
be the Christ, tell us plainly." Jesus answered them,
"I told you, and ye believed not: the works that I do in
my Father's name, they bear witness of me. But ye
believe not, because ye are not of my sheep, as I said
unto you. My sheep hear my voice, and I know them,
and they follow me: and I give unto them eternal life,
and they shall never perish, neither shall any man pluck
them out of my hand. My Father, which gave them me,
is greater than all; and no man is able to pluck them out
of my Father's hand. I and my Father are one."

Then again the Jews picked up stones to stone him.
Jesus answered them, "Many good works have I shewed
you from my Father; for which of those works do ye
stone me?" The Jews answered him, "For a good work
we stone thee not; but for blasphemy; and because that
thou, being a man, makest thyself God." Jesus answered
them, "Is it not written in your law, I said, Ye are gods?
If he called them gods, unto whom the word of God
came, and the scripture cannot be broken; say ye of
him, whom the Father hath sanctified, and sent into the
world, Thou blasphemest; because I said, I am the Son
of God? If I do not the works of my Father, believe
me not. But if I do, though ye believe not me, believe
the works: that you may know, and believe, that the
Father is in me, and I in him."

They tried again to seize him, but he escaped from their grasp, and again went away beyond Jordan to the place where John baptized at first. There he stayed. Many came to him and said, "John did no miracle: but all things that John spoke of this man were true." Then and there they believed in him.

One of the group said to him, "Master, speak to my brother, that he divide the inheritance with me." He said to him, "Man, who made me a judge or a divider over you?"

*The Foolish Rich Man*

And he said to them, "Take heed, and beware of covetousness: for a man's life consisteth not in the abundance of the things which he possesseth." And he spoke a parable to them, saying, "The ground of a certain rich man brought forth plentifully: and he thought within himself, saying, What shall I do, because I have no room where to bestow my fruits? And he said, This will I do: I will pull down my barns, and build greater; and there will I bestow all my fruits and my goods. And I will say to my soul, Soul, thou hast much goods laid up for many years; take thine ease, eat, drink, and be merry. But God said unto him, Thou fool, this night thy soul shall be required of thee: then whose shall those things be, which thou hast provided? So is he that layeth up treasure for himself, and is not rich toward God."

There were present at that time some who told him of the Galileans, whose blood Pilate had mixed with their sacrifices. Jesus answered, "Suppose ye that these Galilaeans were sinners above all the Galilaeans, because they suffered such things? I tell you, Nay: but, except ye repent, ye shall all likewise perish. Or those eighteen, upon whom the tower in Siloam fell, and slew them, think ye that they were sinners above all men that dwelt in Jerusalem? I tell you, Nay: but, except ye repent, ye shall all likewise perish."

*The Galileans Slain by Pilate*

He also spake this parable. "A certain man had a fig tree planted in his vineyard; and he came and sought fruit thereon, and found none. Then said he unto the

| 91

dresser of his vineyard, Behold, these three years I come seeking fruit on this fig tree, and find none: cut it down; why cumbereth it the ground? And he answering said unto him, Lord, let it alone this year also, till I shall dig about it, and dung it: and if it bear fruit, well: and if not, then after that thou shalt cut it down."

*Healing on the Sabbath*

One Sabbath he was teaching in one of the synagogues. There was a woman who had been burdened by an affliction for eighteen years. Her back was bent over and she could not straighten up. When Jesus saw her, he called to her and said, "Woman, thou art loosed from thine infirmity." He laid his hands on her. Immediately she was made straight and she praised God.

The ruler of the synagogue was indignant because Jesus had healed on the Sabbath day. He said to the people, "There are six days in which men ought to work: in them therefore come and be healed, and not on the sabbath day." The Lord then answered him, "Thou hypocrite, doth not each one of you on the sabbath loose his ox or his ass from the stall, and lead him away to watering? And ought not this woman, being a daughter of Abraham, who Satan hath bound, lo, these eighteen years, be loosed from this bond on the sabbath day?"

When he said these things, his opponents were shamed and the people rejoiced because of the glorious things he had done.

*Herod the Fox*

That same day some of the Pharisees came and said to him, "Get thee out, and depart hence: for Herod will kill thee." He said to them, "Go ye, and tell that fox, Behold, I cast out devils, and I do cures to day and to morrow, and the third day I shall be perfected. Nevertheless I must walk to day, and to morrow, and the day following: for it cannot be that a prophet perish out of Jerusalem. O Jerusalem, Jerusalem, which killest the prophets, and stonest them that are sent unto thee; how often would I have gathered thy children together, as a hen doth gather her brood under her

wings, and ye would not! Behold, your house is left unto
you desolate: and verily I say unto you, Ye shall not
see me, until the time come when ye shall say, Blessed
is he that cometh in the name of the Lord."

They watched him as he went to the house of one
of the chief Pharisees to eat on the Sabbath day. There
was a man in front of him who had the dropsy. Jesus
spoke to the lawyers and Pharisees, "Is it lawful to
heal on the sabbath day?" They made no reply. Then
he took hold of him and healed him and let him go, as
he said to them, "Which of you shall have an ass or an
ox fallen into a pit, and will not straightway pull him out
on the sabbath day?" They could not answer this.

He set forth a parable to those who had been invited,
when he noticed how they had chosen the best rooms:
"When thou art bidden of any man to a wedding, sit
not down in the highest room; lest a more honourable
man than thou be bidden of him; and he that bade thee
and him come and say to thee, Give this man place; and
thou begin with shame to take the lowest room. But
when thou art bidden, go and sit down in the lowest
room; that when he that bade thee cometh, he may say
unto thee, Friend, go up higher: then shalt thou have
worship in the presence of them that sit at meat with
thee. For whosoever exalteth himself shall be abased;
and he that humbleth himself shall be exalted."

Then he said to the one who had invited him, "When
thou makest a dinner or a supper, call not thy friends,
nor thy brethren, neither thy kinsmen, nor thy rich
neighbours; lest they also bid thee again, and a recom-
pence be made thee. But when thou makest a feast, call
the poor, the maimed, the lame, the blind: and thou
shalt be blessed; for they cannot recompense thee: for
thou shalt be recompensed at the resurrection of the
just."

When one of those who was sitting at the table
heard these things, he said to him, "Blessed is he that
shall eat bread in the kingdom of God." Then he said

*Parable of the
Great Supper*

to him, "A certain man made a great supper, and bade
many: and sent his servant at supper time to say to
them that were bidden, Come; for all things are now
ready. And they all with one consent began to make
excuses. The first said unto him, I have bought a piece
of ground, and I must needs go and see it: I pray thee
have me excused. And another said, I have bought five
yoke of oxen, and I go to prove them: I pray thee
have me excused. And another said, I have married a wife
and therefore I cannot come. So that servant came, and
shewed his lord these things. Then the master of the
house, being angry said to his servant, Go out quickly
into the streets and the lanes of the city, and bring in
hither the poor and the maimed and the halt and the
blind. And the servant said, Lord, it is done as thou
hast commanded, and yet there is room. And the lord
said unto the servant, Go out into the highways and
hedges, and compel them to come in, that my house
may be filled. For I say unto you, That none of those
men which were bidden shall taste of my supper."

*On Counting
the Cost*

Large crowds went with him. He turned and
said to them, "If any man come to me, and hate not his
father, and mother, and wife, and children, and brethren
and sisters, yea, and his own life also, he cannot be my
disciple. And whosoever doth not bear his cross, and
come after me, cannot be my disciple. For which of you
intending to build a tower, sitteth not down first, and
counteth the cost, whether he have sufficient to finish it?
Lest haply, after he hath laid the foundation, and is not
able to finish it, all that behold it begin to mock him,
saying, This man began to build, and was not able to
finish. Or what king, going to make war against another
king, sitteth not down first, and consulteth whether he
be able with ten thousand to meet him that cometh
against him with twenty thousand? Or else, while the
other is yet a great way off, he sendeth an ambassage and
desireth conditions of peace. So likewise, whosoever h

...e of you that forsaketh not all that he hath, he cannot
...e my disciple."

The tax-gatherers and sinners came close to *The Lost*
...ear him. The Pharisees and scribes complained, "This *Sheep*
...an receiveth sinners, and eateth with them."

And he spoke this parable to them: "What man of you,
...aving an hundred sheep, if he lose one of them, doth not
...eave the ninety and nine in the wilderness, and go after
...hat which is lost, until he find it? And when he hath
...ound it, he layeth it on his shoulders, rejoicing. And
...hen he cometh home, he calleth together his friends
...nd neighbours, saying unto them, Rejoice with me; for
...have found my sheep which was lost. I say unto you,
...hat likewise joy shall be in heaven over one sinner that
...epenteth, more than over ninety and nine just persons,
...which need no repentance.

"Either what woman having ten pieces of *The Lost Coin*
...ilver, if she lose one piece, doth not light a candle, and
...weep the house, and seek diligently till she find it? And
...when she hath found it, she calleth her friends and her
...neighbours together, saying, Rejoice with me; for I have
...found the piece which I had lost. Likewise, I say unto you,
...here is joy in the presence of the angels of God over
...one sinner that repenteth."

And he said, "A certain man had two sons: *The Prodigal*
...and the younger of them said to his father, Father, give *Son*
...me the portion of goods that falleth to me. And he divided
...unto them his living. And not many days after, the
...younger son gathered all together, and took his journey
...into a far country, and there wasted his substance with
...riotous living. And when he had spent all, there arose a
...mighty famine in that land; and he began to be in want.
...And he went and joined himself to a citizen of that coun-
...try; and he sent him into his fields to feed swine. And he
...would fain have filled his belly with the husks that the
...swine did eat: and no man gave unto him. And when he
...came to himself, he said, How many hired servants of

my father's have bread enough and to spare, and I perish
with hunger! I will arise and go to my father, and will
say unto him, Father, I have sinned against heaven, and
before thee, and am no more worthy to be called thy
son: make me as one of thy hired servants.

"And he arose, and came to his father. But when he
was yet a great way off, his father saw him, and had
compassion, and ran, and fell on his neck and kissed him.
And the son said unto him, Father, I have sinned against
heaven and in thy sight, and am no more worthy to be
called thy son. But the father said to his servants, Bring
forth the best robe, and put it on him; and put a ring on
his hand, and shoes on his feet: and bring hither the
fatted calf, and kill it; and let us eat, and be merry: for
this my son was dead, and is alive again; he was lost, and
is found. And they began to be merry.

"Now his elder son was in the field: and as he came
and drew nigh to the house, he heard musick and danc-
ing. And he called one of the servants, and asked what
these things meant. And he said unto him, Thy brother
is come; and thy father hath killed the fatted calf, because
he hath received him safe and sound. And he was angry,
and would not go in: therefore came his father out, and
intreated him. And he answering said to his father, Lo
these many years do I serve thee, neither transgressed
I at any time thy commandment: and yet thou never
gavest me a kid, that I might make merry with my friends:
but as soon as this thy son was come, which hath devoured thy living with harlots, thou hast killed for him
the fatted calf. And he said unto him, Son, thou art ever
with me, and all that I have is thine. It was meet that we
should make merry, and be glad: for this thy brother
was dead, and is alive again, and was lost, and is found."

*Parable of the*
*Unjust*
*Steward*

96 |

He said to his disciples, "There was a certain
rich man, which had a steward; and the same was ac-
cused unto him that he had wasted his goods. And he
called him, and said unto him, How is it that I hear this

of thee? give an account of thy stewardship; for thou mayest be no longer steward. Then the steward said within himself, What shall I do? for my lord taketh away from me the stewardship: I cannot dig; to beg I am ashamed. I am resolved what to do, that, when I am put out of the stewardship, they may receive me into their houses. So he called every one of his lord's debtors unto him, and said unto the first, How much owest thou unto my lord? And he said, An hundred measures of oil. And he said unto him, Take thy bill, and sit down quickly, and write fifty. Then said he to another, And how much owest thou? And he said, An hundred measures of wheat. And he said unto him, Take thy bill, and write four score. And the lord commended the unjust steward, because he had done wisely: for the children of this world are in their generation wiser than the children of light.

"And I say unto you, Make to yourselves friends of the mammon of unrighteousness; that, when ye fail, they may receive you into everlasting habitations. He that is faithful in that which is least is faithful also in much: and he that is unjust in the least is unjust also in much. If therefore ye have not been faithful in the unrighteous mammon, who will commit to your trust the true riches? And if ye have not been faithful in that which is another man's, who shall give you that which is your own?"

The Pharisees, who were also covetous, heard all these things and they scoffed at him. He said to them, "Ye are they which justify yourselves before men; but God knoweth your hearts: for that which is highly esteemed among men is abomination in the sight of God."

"There was a certain rich man, which was *The Rich Man* clothed in purple and fine linen, and fared sumptuously *and Lazarus* every day: and there was a certain beggar named Lazarus, which was laid at his gate, full of sores, and desiring to be fed with the crumbs which fell from the rich man's table: moreover the dogs came and licked his sores. And it came to pass, that the beggar died, and was carried by the angels into Abraham's bosom: the rich man also died, and was buried; and in hell he lift up his eyes, being in torments, and seeth Abraham afar off, and Lazarus in his bosom. And he cried and said, Father Abraham, have mercy on me, and send Lazarus, that he may dip the tip of his finger in water, and cool my tongue; for I am tormented in this flame. But Abraham said, Son, remember that thou in thy lifetime receivedst thy good things, and likewise Lazarus evil things: but now he is comforted, and thou art tormented. And beside all this, between us and you there is a great gulf fixed: so that they which would pass from hence to you cannot; neither can they pass to us, that would come from thence. Then he said, I pray thee therefore, father, that thou wouldest send him to my father's house: for I have five brethren; that he may testify unto them, lest they also come into this place of torment. Abraham saith unto him, They have Moses and the prophets; let them hear them. And he said, Nay, father Abraham: but if one went unto them from the dead, they will repent. And he said unto him, If they hear not Moses and the prophets, neither will they be persuaded, though one rose from the dead."

*Increase Our*
*Faith*

The apostles said to the Lord, "Increase our faith." The Lord said, "If ye had faith as a grain of mustard seed, ye might say unto this sycamine tree, Be thou plucked up by the root, and be thou planted in the sea; and it should obey you. But which of you, having a servant ploughing or feeding cattle, will say unto him by and by, when he is come from the field, Go and sit down to meat? And will not rather say unto him, Make ready wherewith I may sup, and gird thyself, and serve me, till I have eaten and drunken; and afterward thou shalt eat and drink? Doth he thank that servant because he did the things that were commanded him? I trow not. So likewise ye, when ye shall have done all those things which are commanded you, say, We are unprofitable servants; we have done that which was our duty to do."

## The Year
## of Opposition

There was a man named Lazarus who was sick. He was the brother of Mary and Martha, who lived in Bethany. The sisters sent word to Jesus, "Lord, behold, he whom thou lovest is sick." When Jesus heard that, he said, "This sickness is not unto death, but for the glory of God, that the Son of God might be glorified thereby."

Jesus loved Martha and her sister and Lazarus. Therefore, when he heard that he was sick, he remained two days in the same place where he was. Then he said to his disciples, "Let us go into Judea again." His disciples said to him, "Master, the Jews of late sought to stone thee; and goest thou thither again?" Jesus answered, "Are there not twelve hours in the day? If any man walk in the day, he stumbleth not, because he seeth the light of this world. But if a man walk in the night, he stumbleth, because there is no light in him."

Then he added, "Our friend Lazarus sleepeth; but I go, that I may awake him out of sleep." Then his disciples said, "Lord, if he sleep, he shall do well." Jesus had been speaking of his death, but they thought he meant resting through natural sleep. Then Jesus plainly said to them, "Lazarus is dead. And I am glad for your sakes that I was not there, to the intent ye may believe; nevertheless let us go unto him." Then said Thomas, which is called Didymus, to his fellow disciples, "Let us also go, that we may die with him."

When Jesus came, he found that Lazarus had been buried four days already. Bethany was near Jerusalem, about two miles away, and many of the Jews came to Martha and Mary to comfort them about their brother's death.

As soon as Martha heard that Jesus was coming, she went and met him, but Mary stayed in the house. Martha said to Jesus, "Lord, if thou hadst been here, my brother had not died. But I know, that even now, whatsoever thou wilt ask of God, God will give it thee." Jesus said

THE LIFE
OF CHRIST

THE LIFE
OF CHRIST

to her, "Thy brother shall rise again." Martha said to
him, "I know that he shall rise again in the resurrection
at the last day." Jesus said to her, "I am the resurrection,
and the life: he that believeth in me, though he were
dead, yet shall he live: and whosoever liveth and believeth
in me shall never die. Believest thou this?" She saith unto
him, "Yea, Lord: I believe that thou art the Christ, the
Son of God, which should come into the world."

With these words she went and called Mary apart and
told her, "The Master is come, and calleth for thee." As
soon as she heard that, she got up quickly and came to
him.

Jesus had not yet come into the town, but had remained in the place where Martha met him. When the
Jews, which had come to the house and comforted her,
saw Mary hastily leave, they followed her, saying, "She
goeth unto the grave to weep there."

When Mary arrived where Jesus was and saw him, she
knelt at his feet and said to him, "Lord, if thou hadst been
here, my brother had not died." When Jesus saw her
weeping and the Jews who came with her, weeping also,
he sighed deeply and said, "Where have ye laid him?"
They said to him, "Lord, come and see." Jesus wept.
Then the Jews said, "Behold how he loved him!" Some
of them said, "Could not this man, which opened the
eyes of the blind, have caused that even this man should
not have died?"

Again Jesus sighed deeply and came to the grave. It
was a cave and a stone lay in front of it. Jesus said,
"Take ye away the stone." Martha, the dead man's sister,
said to him, "Lord, by this time he stinketh: for he hath
been dead four days." Jesus said to her, "Said I not unto
thee, that, if thou wouldest believe, thou shouldest see the
glory of God?

Then they took the stone away from the grave. Jesus
lifted up his eyes and said, "Father, I thank thee that thou
has heard me. And I knew that thou hearest me always;

but because of the people which stand by I said it, that they may believe that thou hast sent me." When he had said this, he raised his voice and said, "Lazarus, come forth."

The dead man came out, with his hand and feet wrapped in burial linens, and his face wrapped in a napkin. Jesus said to them, "Loose him, and let him go." Then many of the Jews who had come to be with Mary and saw the things which Jesus did, believed in him. But some went to the Pharisees and told them what Jesus had done.

The chief priests and Pharisees gathered for a *Jesus With-*
council and said, "What do we? for this man doeth many *draws to*
miracles. If we let him thus alone, all men will believe on *Ephrain*
him; and the Romans shall come and take away both our place and nation." One of them by the name of Caiaphas, who was high priest that year, said to them, "Ye know nothing at all, nor consider that it is expedient for us, that one man should die for all the people, and that the whole nation perish not." He was not speaking merely for himself, but as the high priest. He was saying that Jesus would die, not only for the nation, but to gather together all the scattered children of God.

From then on they plotted to put him to death. After this, Jesus did not any longer walk openly among the Jews, but went to a country close to the wilderness to a city called Ephrain, and there stayed with his disciples.

Later, as he went to Jerusalem, he passed *The Ten*
through the midst of Samaria and Galilee. As he entered *Lepers*
a certain village, ten men that were lepers met him. They stood back a good distance and called to him, "Jesus, Master, have mercy on us!" When he saw them he told them, "Go shew yourselves unto the priests." It happened as they went, they were cleansed.

When one of them saw that he was healed, he turned back and loudly praised God. He felt down on his face at Jesus' feet and thanked him. He was a Samaritan. Jesus said to him, "Were there not ten cleansed? but where are the nine? There are not found that returned to give glory to God, save this stranger." He then said to him, "Arise, go thy way: thy faith hath made thee whole."

*The Impor-*
*tunate Widow*

When the Pharisees demanded of him when the kingdom of God would come, he answered them, "The kingdom of God cometh not with observation: neither shall they say, Lo here! or, lo there! for, behold, the kingdom of God is within you."

He spoke a parable to them to show that man ought to continue to pray and not to lose heart: "There was in a city a judge, which feared not God, neither regarded man: and there was a widow in that city; and she came unto him, saying, Avenge me of mine adversary. And he would not for a while: but afterward he said within himself, Though I fear not God, nor regard man; yet because this widow troubleth me, I will avenge her, lest by her continual coming she weary me." And the Lord said, "Hear what the unjust judge saith. And shall not God avenge his own elect, which cry day and night unto him, though he bear long with them? I tell you that he will avenge them speedily. Nevertheless when the Son of man cometh, shall he find faith on the earth?"

*The Pharisee*
*and the Pub-*
*lican*

And he spoke this parable to certain ones who were self-righteous and looked down upon others: "Two men went up into the temple to pray; the one a Pharisee, and the other a publican. The Pharisee stood and prayed thus with himself, God, I thank thee, that I am not as other men are, extortioners, unjust, adulterers, or even as this publican. I fast twice in the week, I give tithes of all that I possess. And the publican, standing afar off, would not lift up so much as his eyes unto heaven, but smote upon his breast, saying, God be merciful to me a sinner. I tell you, this man went down to his house justified rather than the other: for every one that exalteth himself shall be abased; and he that humbleth himself shall be exalted."

## The Year
## of Opposition

The Pharisees came testing him by asking, *Marriage and* "Is it lawful for a man to put away his wife for every *Divorce* cause?" He answered, "Have ye not read, that he which made them at the beginning made them male and female, and said, For this cause shall a man leave father and mother, and shall cleave to his wife: and they twain shall be one flesh? Wherefore they are no more twain, but one flesh. What therefore God hath joined together, let not man put asunder." They said to him, "Why did Moses then command to give a writing of divorcement, and to put her away?" He said to them, "Moses because of the hardness of your hearts suffered you to put away your wives: but from the beginning it was not so. And I say unto you, Whosoever shall put away his wife, except it be for fornication, and shall marry another, committeth adultery: and whose marrieth her which is put away doth commit adultery." His disciples said to him, "If the case of the man be so with his wife, it is not good to marry." But he said to them, "All men cannot receive this saying, save they to whom it is given. For there are some eunuchs, which were so born from their mother's womb: and there are some eunuchs, which were made eunuchs of men: and there be eunuchs, which have made themselves eunuchs for the kingdom of heaven's sake. He that is able to receive it, let him receive it."

They brought young children for him to *Jesus Blessing* touch them. His disciples scolded those that brought *Little Children* them. But when Jesus saw it, he was displeased and said to them, "Suffer the little children to come unto me, and forbid them not: for of such is the kingdom of God. Verily I say unto you, Whosoever shall not receive the kingdom of God as a little child, he shall not enter therein." He took them up in his arms, put his hands upon them, and blessed them.

A certain ruler came and said to him, "Good *The Rich* Master, what good thing shall I do, that I may have *Young Ruler* eternal life?" He said to him, "Why callest thou me good? there is none good but one, that is, God: but if thou wilt enter into life, keep the commandments." He asked him, "Which?" Jesus said, "Thou shalt do no murder, Thou shalt not commit adultery, Thou shalt not steal, Thou shalt not bear false witness, Honour thy father and thy mother: and, Thou shalt love thy neighbour as thyself." The young man said to him, "All these things have I kept from my youth up: what lack I yet?" Jesus said to him, "If thou wilt be perfect, go and sell that thou hast, and give to the poor, and thou shalt have treasure in heaven: and come and follow me." But when the young man heard what Jesus said, he went away with a heavy heart, for he was very wealthy.

Then said Jesus to his disciples, "Verily I say unto you, That a rich man shall hardly enter into the kingdom of heaven. And again I say unto you, It is easier for a camel to go through the eye of a needle, than for a rich man to enter into the kingdom of God." When his disciples heard that, they were very astonished and said to him, "Who then can be saved?" Jesus looked at them and said, "With men this is impossible; but with God all things are possible." Peter spoke up and said, "Behold, we have forsaken all, and followed thee; what shall we have therefore?" Jesus said to them, "Verily I say unto you, That ye which have followed me, in the regeneration when the Son of man shall sit in the throne of his glory, ye also shall sit upon twelve thrones, judging the twelve tribes of Israel. And every one that hath forsaken houses, or brethren, or sisters, or father, or mother, or wife, or children, or lands, for my name's sake, shall receive an hundredfold, and shall inherit everlasting life. But many that are first shall be last; and the last shall be first.

"For the kingdom of heaven is like unto a man that is an householder, which went out early in the morning to hire labourers into his vineyard. And when he had agreed with the labourers for a penny a day, he sent them into his vineyard. And he went out about the third hour, and saw others standing idle in the marketplace, and said unto them, Go ye also into the vineyard, and whatsoever is right I will give you. And they went their way. Again he went out about the sixth and ninth hour, and did likewise. And about the eleventh hour he went out, and found others standing idle, and saith unto them, Why stand ye here all the day idle? They say unto him, Because no man hath hired us. He saith unto them, Go ye also into the vineyard; and whatsoever is right, that shall ye receive. So when even was come, the lord of the vineyard saith unto his steward, Call the labourers, and give them their hire, beginning from the last unto the first. And when they came that were hired about the eleventh hour, they received every man a penny. But when the first came, they supposed that they should have received more; and they likewise received every man a penny. And when they had received it, they murmured against the good man of the house, saying, These last have wrought but one hour, and thou hast made them equal unto us, which have borne the burden and heat of the day. But he answered one of them, and said, Friend, I do thee no wrong: didst not thou agree with me for a penny? Take that thine is, and go thy way: I will give unto this last, even as unto thee. Is it not lawful for me to do what I will with mine own? Is thine eye evil, because I am good? So the last shall be first, and the first last: for many are called, but few chosen."

They were on the way to Jerusalem and Jesus went before them. They were both amazed and afraid. *Christ Fore-tells His Death* He took the twelve aside and began to tell them what would happen to him: "All things that are written by the prophets concerning the Son of man shall be accomplished. Behold, we go up to Jerusalem; and the Son of man shall be delivered unto the chief priests, and unto the scribes; and they shall condemn him to death, and shall deliver him to the Gentiles: and they shall mock him, and shall scourge him, and shall spit upon him,

and shall kill him: and the third day he shall rise again."
They did not understand any of this; its meaning was
concealed from them.

*The Request
of James and
John*

James and John, the sons of Zebedee, came
to him and said, "Master, we would that thou shouldest
do for us whatsoever we shall desire." He said to them,
"What would ye that I should do for you?" They said
to him, "Grant unto us that we may sit, one on thy
right hand, and the other on thy left hand, in thy glory."
But Jesus said to them, "Ye know not what ye ask: can
ye drink of the cup that I drink of? and be baptized
with the baptism that I am baptized with?" They said
unto him, "We can." And Jesus said to them, "Ye shall
indeed drink of the cup that I drink of; and with the baptism that I am baptized withal shall ye be baptized: but
to sit on my right hand and on my left hand is not mine
to give; but it shall be given to them for whom it is
prepared."

When the other ten heard it, they were very displeased
with James and John. But Jesus called them to him and
told them, "Ye know that they which are accounted to
rule over the Gentiles exercise lordship over them; and
their great ones exercise authority upon them. But so
shall it not be among you: but whosoever will be great
among you, shall be your minister: and whosoever of you
will be the chiefest, shall be servant of all. For even the
Son of man came not to be ministered unto, but to minister, and to give his life a ransom for many."

*Blind Barti-
maeus Healed*

They came to Jericho. As he left Jericho, with
his disciples and a large number of people, blind Barti-
maeus, the son of Timaeus, sat begging by the side of the
highway. Hearing the multitude go by, he asked what
was going on. They told him that Jesus of Nazareth was
passing by. When he heard that it was Jesus of Nazareth,
he began to cry out, "Jesus, thou son of David, have
mercy on me!" Many told him that he should keep quiet;
but he cried out even more, "Thou son of David, have

106 |

mercy on me!" Jesus stood still and commanded that he be called. They called the blind man and said to him, "Be of good comfort, rise; he calleth thee." Throwing aside his cloak, he stood up and came to Jesus. Jesus said to him, "What wilt thou that I should do unto thee?" The blind man said to him, "Lord, that I might receive my sight." Jesus said to him, "Go thy way; thy faith hath made thee whole." Immediately he received his sight and praised God, as he followed Jesus on the road. When they saw it, all the people gave praise to God.

Jesus entered Jericho and went on through *Zacchaeus* the town. There was a wealthy man there named Zacchaeus, who was the chief tax collector. He made an effort to see Jesus and what he was like, but could not for the crowd of people, for he was a short man. He ran ahead and climbed up into a sycamore tree so he could see him, for he was to pass that way.

When Jesus came to that place, he looked up and saw him, and said to him, "Zacchaeus, make haste, and come down; for today I must abide at thy house." He hurried down and joyfully received him. When the people saw it, they disapproved, saying that he had gone to be the guest of a man that was a sinner.

Zacchaeus stood before the Lord and said to him, "Behold, Lord, the half of my goods I give to the poor; and if I have taken any thing from any man by false accusation, I restore him fourfold." Jesus said to him, "This day is salvation come to this house, forsomuch as he also is a son of Abraham. For the Son of man is come to seek and to save that which was lost."

As the people heard this conversation, he told *The Parable of* them a parable, because he was near Jerusalem and be- *the Pounds* cause they thought the kingdom of God would immediately appear. Therefore he said, "A certain nobleman went into a far country to receive for himself a kingdom, and to return. And he called his ten servants, and delivered them ten pounds, and said unto them, Occupy till

| 107

I come. But his citizens hated him, and sent a message after him, saying, We will not have this man to reign over us. And it came to pass, that when he was returned, having received the kingdom, then he commanded these servants to be called unto him, to whom he had given the money, that he might know how much every man had gained by trading. Then came the first, saying, Lord, thy pound hath gained ten pounds. And he said unto him, Well, thou good servant: because thou hast been faithful in a very little, have thou authority over ten cities. And the second came, saying, Lord, thy pound hath gained five pounds. And he said likewise to him, Be thou also over five cities. And another came, saying, Lord, behold, here is thy pound, which I have kept laid up in a napkin: for I feared thee, because thou art an austere man: thou takest up that thou layedst not down and reapest that thou didst not sow. And he said unto him, Out of thine own mouth will I judge thee, thou wicked servant. Thou knowest that I was an austere man, taking up that I laid not down, and reaping that I did not sow: wherefore then gavest not thou my money into the bank, that at my coming I might have required mine own with usury? And he said unto them that stood by, Take from him the pound, and give it to him that hath ten pounds. And they said unto him, Lord, he hath ten pounds. For I say unto you, That unto every one which hath shall be given; and from him that hath not, even that he hath shall be taken away from him. But those mine enemies, which would not that I should reign over them, bring hither, and slay them before me."

When he had told this, he went forward up the hill toward Jerusalem.

The Jewish Passover was near and many went from the country to Jerusalem to purify themselves before the Passover. They looked for Jesus and talked among themselves as they stood in the temple, saying, "What think ye, that he will not come to the feast?" Both the chief priests and the Pharisees had issued an order that if any man knew where he was, he should tell it, so that they might arrest him.

Six days before the Passover, Jesus came to Bethany, where Lazarus lived, whom he had raised from the dead. They fixed supper for him. Martha served and Lazarus was of the ones who sat at the table with him. Then Mary took a pound of very costly perfume, oil of pure nard, poured it over the feet of Jesus and wiped them with her hair. The house was filled with the odour of the ointment. *Mary and Martha*

Then Judas Iscariot, one of his disciples, the son of Simon and the one who would betray him, said, "Why was not this ointment sold for three hundred pence, and given to the poor?" He said this, not because he cared for the poor but because he was a thief and carried the money bag. Jesus replied, "Let her alone: against the day of my burying hath she kept this. For the poor always ye have with you; but me ye have not always. She hath done what she could: she is come aforehand to anoint my body to the burying. Verily I say unto you, wheresoever this gospel shall be preached throughout the whole world, this also that she hath done shall be spoken of for a memorial of her."

Many of the Jewish people knew he was there and they came, not only to see Jesus, but also to see Lazarus whom he had raised from the dead. The chief priests talked together about putting Lazarus to death because he was the reason that many of the Jews believed in Jesus.

# THE WEEK
# CHRIST DIED

## ✛ *Sunday*

*The Tri-
umphal Entry*
When Jesus came to the Mount of Olives, near Bethphage and Bethany, he sent two of his disciples, instructing them, "Go ye into the village over against you; in the which at your entering ye shall find a colt tied, whereon yet never man sat: loose him, and bring him hither. And if any man ask you, Why do ye loose him? thus shall ye say unto him, Because the Lord hath need of him, and straightway he will send him." This was done in order to fulfill the word of the prophet:

> "Tell ye the daughter of Sion,
> Behold, thy King cometh unto thee,
> Meek, and sitting upon an ass,
> And a colt the foal of an ass."

The two went and found it as he had told them. As they were untying the colt, the owners of it said to them, "Why loose ye the colt?" They replied, "The Lord hath need of him."

They brought him to Jesus, threw their cloaks on him, and set Jesus upon him. As he went, many people who had come to the feast, when they heard Jesus was coming to Jerusalem gathered branches of palm trees and went out to meet him. They cried, "Hosanna: Blessed is the King of Israel that cometh in the name of the Lord."

The people who had been with him when he called Lazarus out of his grave gave testimony of what he had done. This caused many to meet him because they had heard about his miracle. The Pharisees said to each other, "Perceive ye how ye prevail nothing? Behold, the world is gone after him." The people spread their coats on the road. When he was drawing near, even at the foot of the Mount of Olives, the large multitude of his followers began to rejoice and shout praises to God for all the mighty works they had seen him do, saying,

"Hosanna, Blessed be the King that cometh in the name of the Lord; peace in heaven, and glory in the highest!

"Blessed be the kingdom of our father David, that cometh in the name of the Lord. Hosanna in the highest!"

Some of the Pharisees in the crowd said to him, "Master, rebuke thy disciples." He answered them, "I tell you that, if these should hold their peace, the stones would immediately cry out."

When he came near, he saw the city and wept over it. He said, "If thou hadst known, even thou, at least in this thy day, the things which belong unto thy peace! but now they are hid from thine eyes. For the days shall come upon thee, that thine enemies shall cast a trench about thee, and compass thee round, and keep thee in on every side, and shall lay thee even with the ground, and thy children within thee; and they shall not leave in thee one stone upon another; because thou knewest not the time of thy visitation." And when he was come into Jerusalem, all the city was moved, saying, "Who is this?" And the multitude said, "This is Jesus the prophet of Nazareth of Galilee."

Jesus entered Jerusalem and went into the Temple. He looked around at everything there and at dusk, he went out to Bethany with the twelve.

# ✠ *Monday*

*The Fig Tree
Cursed*

The next day, after he had left Bethany, he felt hungry. He saw a fig tree some distance away which had leaves, and he went to it, hoping he might find figs on it. When he came to it, he found nothing but leaves for it was not yet the season for figs. Jesus said to the tree, "No man eat fruit of thee hereafter for ever." The disciples heard what he said.

*The Cleansing
of the Temple*

The time for the Jews' Passover was near, and Jesus went to Jerusalem. He found people in the temple who sold oxen, sheep, and doves; and also moneychangers. When he had made a whip of small cords, he drove them all out of the temple, including the sheep and oxen, and he poured out the changers' money and overturned their tables. He said to those who sold doves, "Take these things hence; make not my Father's house an house of merchandise." He would not permit any man to carry a vessel through the temple. He told them, "Is it not written, My house shall be called of all nations the house of prayer? but ye have made it a den of thieves." The scribes and chief priests heard it and looked for a way to destroy him. They were afraid, on account of all the people being impressed with his words. They could not do anything, however, because all the people were close around in order to hear him. Blind and crippled people came to him in the temple and he healed them. When the chief priests and scribes saw the wonderful things which he did, and heard the people in the temple saying, "Hosanna to the Son of David!" they were very displeased and said to him, "Hearest thou what these say?" Jesus said to them, "Yea; have ye never read, Out of the mouth of babes and sucklings thou hast perfected praise?" His disciples remembered that it was written, "The zeal of thine house hath eaten me up."

Then the Jews said to him, "What sign shewest thou

unto us, seeing that thou doest these things?" Jesus answered, "Destroy this temple, and in three days I will raise it up." Then the Jews said, "Forty and six years was this temple in building, and wilt thou rear it up in three days?" But he spoke of his body as the temple. Later when he had risen from the dead, his disciples remembered that he had said this to them and they believed the scripture and what Jesus had said. He left them and went away from the city to Bethany and spent the night there.

## ✠ *Tuesday and Wednesday*

As they passed by the next morning, they saw the fig tree was withered from the roots up. Peter, remembering what Jesus had said to the tree, said to him, "Master, behold, the fig tree which thou cursedst is withered away." Jesus answered, "Have faith in God. For verily I say unto you, That whosoever shall say unto this mountain, Be thou removed and be thou cast into the sea; and shall not doubt in his heart, but shall believe that those things which he saith shall come to pass; he shall have whatsoever he saith. Therefore I say unto you, what things soever ye desire, when ye pray, believe that ye receive them, and ye shall have them." *The Fig Tree Withered*

They came again to Jerusalem. As he was walking into the temple, the chief priests and the scribes and the elders said to him, "By what authority doest thou these things? and who gave thee this authority to do these things?" Jesus answered, "I will also ask of you one question, and answer me, and I will tell you by what authority I do these things. The baptism of John, was it from heaven, or of men? answer me." They talked among themselves, saying, "If we shall say, From heaven; he will say, Why then did ye not believe him? But if we shall say, Of men . . ."—they feared the people, for all men counted John as a prophet indeed. And they said to *The Authority of Jesus Challenged*

| 113

Jesus, "We cannot tell." And Jesus answered, "Neither do I tell you by what authority I do these things."

*The Parable of the Two Sons*

He went on to say to them, "But what think ye? A certain man had two sons; and he came to the first, and said, Son, go work to day in my vineyard. He answered and said, I will not: but afterward he repented, and went. And he came to the second, and said likewise. And he answered and said, I go, sir: and went not. Whether of them twain did the will of his father?" They say unto him, "The first." Jesus saith unto them, "Verily I say unto you, That the publicans and the harlots go into the kingdom of God before you. For John came unto you in the way of righteousness, and ye believed him not: but the publicans and the harlots believed him: and ye, when ye had seen it, repented not afterward, that ye might believe him.

*The Wicked Husbandmen*

"Hear another parable: There was a certain householder, which planted a vineyard, and hedged it round about, and digged a winepress in it, and built a tower, and let it out to husbandmen, and went into a far country: and when the time of the fruit drew near, he sent his servants to the husbandmen, that they might receive the fruits of it. And the husbandmen took his servants, and beat one, and killed another, and stoned another. Again, he sent other servants more than the first: and they did unto them likewise. But last of all he sent unto them his son, saying, They will reverence my son. But when the husbandmen saw the son, they said among themselves, This is the heir; come, let us kill him, and let us seize on his inheritance. And they caught him, and cast him out of the vineyard, and slew him. When the lord therefore of the vineyard cometh, what will he do unto those husbandmen?" They said to him, "He will miserably destroy those wicked men, and will let out his vineyard unto other husbandmen, which shall render him the fruits in their seasons." Jesus said to them, "Did ye never read in the scriptures,

> The stone which the builders rejected,
> The same is become the head of the corner:
> This is the Lord's doing,
> And it is marvellous in our eyes?

Therefore say I unto you, the kingdom of God shall be taken from you, and given to a nation bringing forth the fruits thereof. And whosoever shall fall on this stone shall be broken: but on whomsoever it shall fall, it will grind him to powder."

They wanted to arrest him, but were afraid of the people; because they knew he had spoken the parable against them.

Jesus spoke to them again through parables: *The Marriage* "The kingdom of heaven is like unto a certain king, *Feast of the* which made a marriage for his son, and sent forth his *King's Son* servants to call them that were bidden to the wedding: and they would not come. Again, he sent forth other servants, saying, Tell them which are bidden, Behold, I have prepared my dinner: my oxen and my fatlings are killed, and all things are ready: come unto the marriage. But they made light of it, and went their ways, one to his farm, another to his merchandise: and the remnant took his servants, and entreated them spitefully, and slew them. But when the king heard thereof, he was wroth: and he sent forth his armies, and destroyed those murderers, and burned up their city. Then saith he to his servants, The wedding is ready, but they which were bidden were not worthy. Go ye therefore into the highways, and as many as ye shall find, bid to the marriage. So those servants went out into the highways, and gathered together all as many as they found, both bad and good: and the wedding was furnished with guests. And when the king came in to see the guests, he saw there a man which had not on a wedding garment: and he saith unto him, Friend, how camest thou in hither not having a wedding garment? And he was speechless. Then said the king to the servants,

Bind him hand and foot, and take him away, and cast him into outer darkness; there shall be weeping and gnashing of teeth. For many are called, but few are chosen."

*Tribute to Caesar?*

Then the Pharisees went and talked together as to how they might trap him with his own words. They sent some of their followers in company with Herodians, and said to him, "Master, we know that thou art true, and teachest the way of God in truth, neither carest thou for any man: for thou regardest not the person of men. Tell us therefore, What thinkest thou? Is it lawful to give tribute unto Caesar, or not?" But Jesus realized their evil intentions and said, "Why tempt ye me, ye hypocrites? Shew me the tribute money." They brought to him a penny. He said to them, "Whose is this image and superscription?" They replied, "Caesar's." Then he said to them, "Render therefore unto Caesar the things which are Caesar's; and unto God the things that are God's." When they had heard these words, they were taken by surprise and they went away and left him.

*Is There a Resurrection?*

The Sadducees came to him that same day, saying there is no resurrection, and said to him, "Master, Moses said, If a man die, having no children, his brother shall marry his wife, and raise up seed unto his brother. Now there were with us seven brethren: and the first, when he had married a wife, deceased, and, having no issue, left his wife unto his brother: likewise the second also, and the third, unto the seventh. And last of all the woman died also. Therefore in the resurrection whose wife shall she be of the seven? for they all had her." Jesus answered and said to them, "Ye do err, not knowing the scriptures nor the power of God. For in the resurrection they neither marry, nor are given in marriage, but are as the angels of God in heaven. But as touching the resurrection of the dead, have ye not read in the book of Moses, how in the bush that which was spoken unto you by God, saying, I am the God of Abraham, and the God

116 |

of Isaac, and the God of Jacob? God is not the God of the dead, but of the living." When the multitude heard this, they were astounded at his teaching.

One of the scribes came and hearing their discussions together, and realizing that Jesus had answered them well, asked him, "Which is the first commandment of all?" Jesus answered him, "The first of all the commandments is, Hear, O Israel; the Lord our God is one Lord: and thou shalt love the lord thy God with all thy heart, and with all thy soul, and with all thy mind, and with all thy strength: this is the first commandment. And the second is like, namely this, Thou shalt love thy neighbour as thyself. There is none other commandment greater than these." The scribe said to him, "Well, Master, thou hast said the truth: for there is one God; and there is none other but he: and to love him with all the heart, and with all the understanding, and with all the soul, and with all the strength, and to love his neighbour as himself, is more than all the whole burnt offerings and sacrifices." When Jesus saw how wisely the man answered, he said to him, "Thou art not far from the kingdom of God."

*Which Is the Greatest Commandment?*

While the Pharisees were there together, Jesus asked them, "What think ye of Christ? whose son is he?" They replied, "The son of David." He saith to them, "How doth David in spirit call him Lord, saying,

*Jesus Questions Them*

> The Lord said unto my Lord,
> Sit thou on my right hand,
> Till I make thine enemies thy footstool?

If David then call him Lord, how is he his son?" No man was able to answer him a word and from that day on, no one asked him any more questions.

Jesus then spoke to the multitude and to his disciples, saying, "The scribes and the Pharisees sit in Moses' seat: all therefore whatsoever they bid you observe, that observe and do; but do not ye after their

*Woes Against the Scribes and Pharisees*

| 117

works: for they say, and do not. For they bind heavy burdens and grievous to be borne, and lay them on men's shoulders; but they themselves will not move them with one of their fingers. But all their works they do for to be seen of men: they make broad their phylacteries, and enlarge the borders of their garments, and love the uppermost rooms at feasts, and the chief seats in the synagogues, and greetings in the markets, and to be called of men, Rabbi, Rabbi. But be not ye called Rabbi: for one is your Master, even Christ; and all ye are brethren. And call no man your father upon the earth: for one is your Father, which is in heaven. Neither be ye called masters: for one is your Master, even Christ. But he that is greatest among you shall be your servant. And whosoever shall exalt himself shall be abased; and he that shall humble himself shall be exalted.

"But woe unto you, scribes and Pharisees, hypocrites! for ye shut up the kingdom of heaven against men: for ye neither go in yourselves, neither suffer ye them that are entering to go in.

"Woe unto you, scribes and Pharisees, hypocrites! for ye devour widows' houses, and for a pretence make long prayer: therefore ye shall receive the greater damnation.

"Woe unto you, scribes and Pharisees, hypocrites! for ye compass sea and land to make one proselyte, and when he is made, ye make him twofold more the child of hell than yourselves.

"Woe unto you, ye blind guides, which say, Whosoever shall swear by the temple, it is nothing; but whosoever shall swear by the gold of the temple, he is a debtor. Ye fools and blind: for whether is greater, the gold, or the temple that sanctifieth the gold? And, Whosoever shall swear by the altar, it is nothing; but whosoever sweareth by the gift that is upon it, he is guilty. Ye fools and blind: for whether is greater, the gift, or the altar that sanctifieth the gift? Whoso therefore shall swear by the altar, sweareth by it, and by all things thereon. And whoso shall swear by the temple, sweareth by it, and by him that dwelleth therein. And he that shall swear by heaven, sweareth by the throne of God, and by him that sitteth thereon.

"Woe unto you, scribes and Pharisees, hypocrites! for ye pay tithe of mint and anise and cummin, and have omitted the weightier matters of the law, judgment, mercy, and faith: these ought ye to have done, and not to leave the other undone. Ye blind guides, which strain at a gnat, and swallow a camel.

"Woe unto you, scribes and Pharisees, hypocrites! for ye make clean the outside of the cup and the platter, but within they are full of extortion and excess. Thou blind Pharisee, cleanse first that which is within the cup and platter, that the outside of them may be clean also.

"Woe unto you, scribes and Pharisees, hypocrites! for ye are like unto whited sepulchres, which indeed appear beautiful outward, but are within full of dead men's bones and of all uncleanness. Even so ye also outwardly appear righteous unto men, but within ye are full of hypocrisy and iniquity.

"Woe unto you, scribes and Pharisees, hypocrites! because ye build the tombs of the prophets, and garnish the sepulchres of the righteous, and say, if we had been in the days of our fathers, we would not have been partakers with them in the blood of the prophets. Wherefore ye be witnesses unto yourselves, that ye are the children of them which killed the prophets. Fill ye up then the measure of your fathers. Ye serpents, ye generation of vipers, how can ye escape the damnation of hell? Wherefore, behold, I send you prophets, and wise men, and scribes: and some of them ye shall kill and crucify; and some of them shall ye scourge in your synagogues, and persecute them from city to city: that upon you may come all the righteous blood shed upon the earth, from the blood of righteous Abel unto the blood of Zacharias, son of Barachias, whom ye slew between the temple and the altar. Verily I say unto you, All these things shall come upon this generation."

**The Widow's
Mites**

Jesus sat near the treasury, watching the people as they put their money into the offering box. Many of the rich gave large amounts. There was a poor widow who came and put in two mites, together making a farthing. He called his disciples to him and said to them, "Verily I say unto you, That this poor widow hath cast more in, than all they which have cast into the treasury: for all they did cast in of their abundance; but she of her want did cast in all that she had, even all her living."

**The Son of
Man**

Some Greeks were among those who came to worship at the festival. They came to Philip, who was from Bethsaida in Galilee, and said to him, "Sir, we would see Jesus." Philip came and told Andrew, and the two of them told Jesus.

Jesus replied, "The hour is come, that the Son of man should be glorified. Verily, verily, I say unto you, Except a corn of wheat fall into the ground and die, it abideth alone: but if it die, it bringeth forth much fruit. He that loveth his life shall lose it; and he that hateth his life in this world shall keep it unto life eternal. If any man serve me, let him follow me; and where I am, there shall also my servant be: if any man serve me, him will my Father honour. Now is my soul troubled; and what shall I say? Father, save me from this hour: but for this cause came I unto this hour. Father, glorify thy name."

Then a voice came from heaven, saying, "I have both glorified it, and will glorify it again." The people standing by said that it thundered, others said, "An angel spake to him." Jesus answered, "This voice came not because of me, but for your sakes. Now is the judgment of this world: now shall the prince of this world be cast out. And I, if I be lifted up from the earth, will draw all men unto me." He said this to signify the death he would die.

The people answered him, "We have heard out of the law that Christ abideth for ever: and how sayest thou,

The Son of man must be lifted up? who is this Son of man?" Then Jesus said to them, "Yet a little while is the light with you. Walk while ye have the light, lest darkness come upon you: for he that walketh in darkness knowest not whither he goeth. While ye have light, believe in the light, that ye may be the children of light." Jesus spoke these things and then went away into hiding. Though he had done many miracles before them, still they did not believe. Thus the prophecy of Isaiah was fulfilled,

"Lord, who hath believed our report?
And to whom hath the arm of the Lord been revealed?"

Therefore they could not believe, because that Esaias said also,

"He hath blinded their eyes, and hardened their heart;
That they should not see with their eyes, nor understand
    with their heart,
And be converted,
And I should heal them."

Esaias said these things when he saw his glory and spoke of him. Nevertheless there were many among these in authority who did believe in him, but because of the Pharisees they did not let it be known. They were afraid of being put out of the synagogue, because they loved the praise of men more than the praise of God.

Jesus said, "He that believeth on me, believeth not on me, but on him that sent me. And he that seeth me seeth him that sent me. I am come a light into the world, that whosoever believeth on me should not abide in darkness. And if any man hear my words, and believe not, I judge him not; for I came not to judge the world, but to save the world. He that rejecteth me, and receiveth not my words, hath one that judgeth him: the word that I have spoken, the same shall judge him in the last day. For I have not spoken of myself; but the Father which sent me,

he gave me a commandment, what I should say, and what
I should speak. And I know that his commandment is life
everlasting: whatsoever I speak therefore, even as the
Father said unto me, so I speak."

*Discourses of
Christ on the
Destruction of
Jerusalem
and the End
of the World*

As they were leaving the temple, Peter, James,
John and Andrew called his attention to the buildings
of the temple. Jesus said to them, "See ye not all these
things? verily I say unto you, There shall not be left
here one stone upon another, that shall not be thrown
down."

As he was sitting on the Mount of Olives, the disciples
said to him in private, "Tell us, when shall these things
be? and what shall be the sign of thy coming, and of the
end of the world?" Jesus answered, "Take heed that no
man deceive you. For many shall come in my name,
saying, I am Christ; and shall deceive many. And ye
shall hear of wars and rumours of wars: see that ye be not
troubled: for all these things must come to pass, but the
end is not yet. For nation shall rise against nation, and
kingdom against kingdom: and there shall be famines,
and pestilences, and earthquakes, in divers places. All these
are the beginning of sorrows. Then shall they deliver you
up to be afflicted, and shall kill you: and ye shall be
hated of all nations for my name's sake. And then shall
many be offended, and shall betray one another, and
shall hate one another. And many false prophets shall
rise, and shall deceive many. And because iniquity shall
abound, the love of many shall wax cold. And the gospel must first be published among all nations. But when
they shall lead you, and deliver you up, take no thought
beforehand what ye shall speak, neither do ye premedi-
tate: but whatsoever shall be given you in that hour, that
speak ye: for it is not ye that speak, but the Holy Ghost.
Now the brother shall betray the brother to death, and
the father the son; and the children shall rise up against
their parents, and shall cause them to be put to death. And
ye shall be hated of all men for my name's sake: but he

that shall endure unto the end, the same shall be saved. In your patience possess ye your souls.

"When ye therefore shall see the abomination of desolation, spoken of by Daniel the prophet, stand in the holy place, (whoso readeth, let him understand:) then let them which be in Judea flee into the mountains: let him which is on the house top not come down to take any thing out of his house: neither let him which is in the field return back to take his clothes. Remember Lot's wife. And woe unto them that are with child, and to them that give suck in those days! But pray ye that your flight be not in the winter, neither on the sabbath day: for then shall be great tribulation, such as was not since the beginning of the world to this time, no, nor ever shall be. And except those days should be shortened, there should no flesh be saved: but for the elect's sake those days shall be shortened. Then if any man shall say unto you, Lo, here is Christ, or there; believe it not. For there shall arise false Christs, and false prophets, and shall shew great signs and wonders; insomuch that, if it were possible, they shall deceive the very elect. Behold, I have told you before. Wherefore if they shall say unto you, Behold, he is in the desert; go not forth: behold, he is in the secret chambers; believe it not. For as the lightning cometh out of the east, and shineth even unto the west; so shall also the coming of the Son of man be. For wheresoever the carcase is, there will the eagles be gathered together.

"Immediately after the tribulation of those days shall the sun be darkened, and the moon shall not give her light, and the stars shall fall from heaven, and the powers of the heavens shall be shaken: and then shall appear the sign of the Son of man in heaven: and then shall all the tribes of the earth mourn, and they shall see the Son of man coming in the clouds of heaven with power and great glory. And he shall send his angels with a great sound of a trumpet, and they shall gather together his elect from the four winds, from one end of heaven to the other. And when these things begin to come to pass, then look up, and lift up your heads; for your redemption draweth nigh.

"Now learn a parable of the fig tree; When his branch is yet tender, and putteth forth leaves, ye know that summer is nigh: So likewise ye, when ye shall see all these things, know that it is near, even at the doors. Verily I say unto you, This generation shall not pass, till all these things be fulfilled. Heaven and earth shall pass away, but my words shall not pass away. But of that day and hour knoweth no man, no, not the angels of heaven, but my Father only. But as the days of Noah were, so shall also the coming of the Son of man be. For as in the days that were before the flood they were eating and drinking, marrying and giving in marriage, until the day that Noah entered into the ark, and knew not until the flood came, and took them all away; so shall also the coming of the Son of man be. Then shall two be in the field; the one shall be taken, and the other left. Two women shall be grinding at the mill; the one shall be taken, and the other left.

"Let your loins be girded about, and your lights burning; and ye yourselves like unto men that wait for their lord, when he will return from the wedding; that when he cometh and knocketh, they may open unto him immediately. Blessed are those servants, whom the lord when he cometh shall find watching: verily I say unto you, that he shall gird himself, and make them to sit down to meat, and will come forth and serve them. And if he shall come in the second watch, or come in the third watch, and find them so, blessed are those servants. Take ye heed, watch and pray: for ye know not when the time is. For the Son of man is as a man taking a far journey, who left his house, and gave authority to his servants, and to every man his work, and commanded the porter to watch. Watch ye therefore: for ye know not when the master of the house cometh, at even, or at midnight, or at the cockcrowing, or in the morning: lest coming suddenly he find you sleeping. And what I say unto you I say unto all, Watch. Watch ye therefore, and pray always, that ye may be accounted worthy to escape all these things that shall come to pass, and to stand before the Son of man. Who then is a faithful and wise servant, whom his lord hath made ruler over his household, to give them meat in due season? Blessed is that servant, whom his lord when he cometh shall find so doing. Verily I say unto you, That he shall make him ruler over all his goods. But and if that evil servant shall say in his heart, My lord delayeth his coming; and shall begin to smite his fellow servants, and to eat and drink with the drunken; the lord of that servant shall come in a day when he looketh not for him, and in an hour that he is not aware of, and shall cut him asunder, and appoint him his portion with the hypocrites: there shall be weeping and gnashing of teeth. And that servant which knew his lord's will, and prepared not himself, neither did according to his will, shall be beaten with many stripes. But he that knew not, and did commit things worthy of stripes, shall be beaten with few stripes. For unto whomsoever much is given, of him shall be much required: and to whom men have committed much, of him they will ask the more.

"Then shall the kingdom of heaven be likened unto ten virgins, which took their lamps, and went forth to meet the bridegroom. And five of them were wise, and five were foolish. They that were foolish took their lamps, and took no oil with them: but the wise took oil in their vessels with their lamps. While the bridegroom tarried, they all slumbered and slept. And at midnight there was a cry made, Behold, the bridegroom cometh; go ye out to meet him. Then all those virgins arose, and trimmed their lamps. And the foolish said unto the wise, Give us of your oil; for our lamps are gone out. But the wise answered, saying, Not so; lest there be not enough for us and you: but go ye rather to them that sell, and buy for yourselves. And while they went to buy, the bridegroom came; and they that were ready went in with him to the marriage: and the door was shut. Afterward came also the other virgins, saying, Lord, Lord, open to us. But he answered and said, Verily I say unto you, I know you not. Watch therefore, for ye know neither the day nor the hour wherein the Son of man cometh.

"For the kingdom of heaven is as a man traveling into a far country, who called his own servants, and delivered unto them his goods. And unto one he gave five talents, and to another two, and to another one; to every man according to his several ability; and straightway took his journey. Then he that had received the five talents went and traded with the same, and made them other five talents. And likewise he that had received two, he also gained other two. But he that had received one went and digged in the earth, and hid his lord's money. After a long time the lord of those servants cometh, and reckoneth with them. And so he that had received five talents came and brought other five talents, saying, Lord, thou deliveredst unto me five talents: behold, I have gained beside them five talents more. His lord said unto him, Well done, thou good and faithful servant: thou hast been faithful over a few things, I will make thee ruler over many things: enter thou into the joy of thy lord. He also that had received two talents came and said, Lord, thou deliveredst unto me two talents: behold, I have gained two other talents beside them. His lord said unto him, Well done, good and faithful servant; thou hast been faithful over a few things, I will make thee ruler over many things: enter thou into the joy of thy lord. Then he which had received the one talent came and said, Lord, I knew thee that thou art an hard man, reaping where thou hast not sown, and gathering where thou hast not strawed: and I was afraid, and went and hid thy talent

in the earth: lo, there thou hast that is thine. His lord
answered and said unto him, Thou wicked and slothful
servant, thou knewest that I reap where I sowed not, and
gather where I have not strawed: thou oughtest therefore
to have put my money to the exchangers, and then at my
coming I should have received mine own with usury. Take
therefore the talent from him, and give it unto him which
hath ten talents. For unto every one that hath shall be
given, and he shall have abundance: but from him that
hath not shall be taken away even that which he hath.
And cast ye the unprofitable servant into outer darkness:
there shall be weeping and gnashing of teeth.

"When the Son of man shall come in his glory, and all
the holy angels with him, then shall he sit upon the throne
of his glory: and before him shall be gathered all nations;
and he shall separate them one from another, as a shepherd
divideth his sheep from the goats: and he shall set the
sheep on his right hand, but the goats on the left. Then
shall the King say unto them on his right hand, Come,
ye blessed of my Father, inherit the kingdom prepared
for you from the foundation of the world: for I was
an hungred, and ye gave me meat: I was thirsty, and ye
gave me drink: I was a stranger, and ye took me in: naked,
and ye clothed me: I was sick, and ye visited me: I was
in prison, and ye came unto me. Then shall the righteous
answer him, saying, Lord, when saw we thee an hungred,
and fed thee? or thirsty, and gave thee drink? When saw
we thee a stranger, and took thee in? or naked, and clothed
thee? Or when saw we thee sick, or in prison, and came
unto thee? And the King shall answer and say unto them,
Verily I say unto you, Inasmuch as ye have done it
unto one of the least of these my brethren, ye have done
it unto me. Then shall he say also unto them on the left
hand, Depart from me, ye cursed, into everlasting fire,
prepared for the devil and his angels: for I was an
hungred, and ye gave me no meat: I was thirsty, and ye
gave me no drink: I was a stranger, and ye took me not

| 127

in: naked, and ye clothed me not: sick, and in prison, and ye visited me not. Then shall they also answer him, saying, Lord, when saw we thee an hungred, or athirst, or a stranger, or naked, or sick, or in prison, and did not minister unto thee? Then shall he answer them, saying, Verily I say unto you, Inasmuch as ye did it not to one of the least of these, ye did it not to me. And these shall go away into everlasting punishment: but the righteous into life eternal."

When Jesus had finished all these sayings, he said to his disciples, "Ye know that after two days is the feast of the passover, and the Son of man is betrayed to be crucified."

*The Bargain of Judas*

The time was near for the feast of unleavened bread, which is the Passover.

The chief priests, scribes and the elders met together in the palace of the high priest, Caiaphas, and schemed as to how they might arrest Jesus by some trick and kill him. They said, however, "Not on the feast day, lest there be an uproar among the people."

Then Satan entered into Judas Iscariot, one of the twelve. He went and talked with the chief priests and officers as to how he might betray him unto them. He asked them, "What will ye give me, and I will deliver him unto you?" They were glad to hear him say this and they made a bargain with him for thirty pieces of silver. From then on he looked for an opportunity to betray him.

# ✠ *Thursday*

*The Last Supper*

Then came the day of unleavened bread, upon which the Passover animal must be slaughtered. Jesus sent Peter and John with instructions: "Go and prepare us the passover, that we may eat." They said to him, "Where wilt thou that we prepare?" And he said unto them,

"Behold, when ye are entered into the city, there shall a man meet you, bearing a pitcher of water; follow him into the house where he entereth in. And ye shall say unto the goodman of the house, The Master saith unto thee, Where is the guestchamber, where I shall eat the passover with my disciples? And he shall shew you a large upper room furnished: there make ready." They went and found everything as he said it would be, and they prepared the Passover.

Before the feast of the Passover, Jesus knew that the time had come when he would depart from this world and go to his Father. He had always loved his own in this world; he would love them until the end. The devil had now put it into the heart of Judas Iscariot, Simon's son, to betray him. Jesus knew that the Father had given him power over all things and that he had come from and would return to God. During supper, he rose, put aside his cloak, took a towel and tied it around himself. He poured water into a basin and began to wash the disciples' feet and to wipe them with the towel.

When he came to Simon Peter, Peter said to him, "Lord, dost thou wash my feet?" Jesus answered, "What I do thou knowest not now; but thou shalt know here-after." Peter said, "Thou shalt never wash my feet." Jesus answered, "If I wash thee not, thou hast no part with me." Simon Peter replied, "Lord, not my feet only, but also my hands and my head." Jesus said to him, "He that is washed needeth not save to wash his feet, but is clean every whit: and ye are clean, but not all." For he knew who was going to betray him; that is why he added, "Ye are not all clean."

After he had washed their feet and re-arranged his clothing, he sat down and said to them, "Know ye what I have done to you? Ye call me Master and Lord: and ye say well; for so I am. If I then, your Lord and Master, have washed your feet; ye also ought to wash one an-other's feet. For I have given you an example, that ye should do as I have done to you. Verily, verily, I say unto you, The servant is not greater than his lord; neither he that is sent greater than he that sent him. If ye know these things, happy are ye if ye do them. I speak not of you all: I know whom I have chosen: but that the scripture be fulfilled, He that eateth bread with me hath lifted up his heel against me. Now I tell you before it come, that, when it is come to pass, ye may believe that I am he. Verily, verily, I say unto you, He that receiveth whomsoever I send receiveth me; and he that receiveth me receiveth him that sent me."

Then, still sitting at the table with the twelve apostles, he said to them, "With desire I have desired to eat this passover with you before I suffer: for I say unto you, I will not any more eat therof, until it be fulfilled in the kingdom of God." And as they ate, he said, "Verily, verily, I say unto you, that one of you shall betray me." They were very sorrowful, and all of them began to say to him, "Lord, is it I?" He answered, "He that dippeth his hand with me in the dish, the same shall betray me. The Son of man goeth as it is written of him: but woe unto that man by whom the Son of man is betrayed! it had been good for that man if he had not been born." Then Judas, who betrayed him, said, "Master, is it I?" He said to him, "Thou hast said." Then said Jesus to him, "That thou doest, do quickly."

None of those at the table knew for what purpose he said this to Judas. Because Judas carried the money, some of them thought that was why Jesus said to him, "Buy those things that we have need of against the feast." Or some thought that he meant that he should give something to the poor. Judas immediately went out. It was night.

After Judas was gone, Jesus said, "Now is the Son of man glorified, and God is glorified in him. If God be glorified in him, God shall also glorify him in himself, and shall straightway glorify him. Little children, yet a little while I am with you. Ye shall seek me: and as I said unto the Jews, Whither I go, ye cannot come; so now I say to you. A new commandment I give unto you, That ye love one another; as I have loved you, that ye also love one another. By this shall all men know that ye are my disciples, if ye have love one to another."

There was a dispute among the disciples as to which of them would be considered the most important. Jesus said to them, "The kings of the Gentiles exercise lordship over them; and they that exercise authority upon them are called benefactors. But ye shall not be so: but he that is greatest among you, let him be as the younger; and he that is chief, as he that doth serve. For whether is greater, he that sitteth at meat, or he that serveth? is not he that sitteth at meat? but I am among you as he that serveth. Ye are they which have continued with me in my temptations. And I appoint unto you a kingdom, as my Father hath appointed unto me; that ye may eat and drink at my table in my kingdom, and sit on thrones judging the twelve tribes of Israel."

Then he took bread, gave thanks, broke it, and passed it to them, saying, "This is my body which is given for you: this do in remembrance of me." Likewise he passed the cup after supper, saying, "This cup is the new testament in my blood, which is shed for you."

After they had sung a hymn, they went out to the Mount of Olives. There Jesus said to them, "All ye shall be offended because of me this night: for it is written, I will smite the shepherd, and the sheep of the flock shall be scattered abroad. But after I am risen again, I will go before you into Galilee." Peter said to him, "Though all men shall be offended because of thee, yet will I never be offended." Jesus said to him, "Verily I say unto thee, That this night, before the cock crow, thou shalt deny me thrice." Peter said to him, "Though I should die with thee, yet I will not deny thee." All the disciples agreed.

*Farewell Discourses*

| 131

He said to them, "When I sent you without purse, and scrip, and shoes, lacked ye any thing?" And they said, "Nothing." Then he said to them, "But now, he that hath a purse, let him take it, and likewise his scrip: and he that hath no sword, let him sell his garment, and buy one. For I say unto you that this that is written must yet be accomplished in me, And he was reckoned among the transgressors: for the things concerning me have an end." They said, "Lord, behold, here are two swords." And he said, "It is enough."

"Let not your heart be troubled: ye believe in God, believe also in me. In my Father's house are many mansions: if it were not so, I would have told you. I go to prepare a place for you. And if I go and prepare a place for you, I will come again, and receive you unto myself; that where I am, there ye may be also. And whither I go ye know, and the way ye know."

Thomas said to him, "Lord, we know not whither thou goest; and how can we know the way?" Jesus said to him, "I am the way, the truth, and the life: no man cometh unto the Father, but by me. If ye had known me, ye should have known my Father also: and from henceforth ye know him, and have seen him."

Philip said, "Lord, shew us the Father, and it sufficeth us." Jesus said, "Have I been so long time with you, and yet hast thou not known me, Philip? He that hath seen me hath seen the Father; and how sayest thou then, Shew us the Father? Believest thou not that I am in the Father, and the Father in me? The words that I speak unto you I speak not of myself: but the Father that dwelleth in me, he doeth the works. Believe me that I am in the Father, and the Father in me: or else believe me for the very works' sake. Verily, verily, I say unto you, He that believeth on me, the works that I do shall he do also; and greater works than these shall he do; because I go unto my Father. And whatsoever ye shall ask in my name, that will I do, that the Father may be glorified in the Son. If ye shall ask any thing in my name,

I will do it. If ye love me, keep my commandments. And I will pray the Father, and he shall give you another Comforter, that he may abide with you for ever; even the Spirit of truth; whom the world cannot receive, because it seeth him not, neither knoweth him: but ye know him; for he dwelleth with you, and shall be in you. I will not leave you comfortless: I will come to you. Yet a little while, and the world seeth me no more; but ye see me: because I live, ye shall live also. At that day ye shall know that I am in my Father, and ye in me, and I in you. He that hath my commandments, and keepeth them, he it is that loveth me: and he that loveth me shall be loved of my Father, and I will love him, and will manifest myself to him."

Judas (not Iscariot), said to him, "Lord, how is it that thou wilt manifest thyself unto us, and not unto the world?" Jesus answered, "If a man love me, he will keep my words: and my Father will love him, and we will come unto him, and make our abode with him. He that loveth me not keepeth not my sayings: and the word which ye hear is not mine, but the Father's which sent me. These things have I spoken unto you, being yet present with you. But the Comforter shall teach you all things, and bring all things to your remembrance, whatsoever I have said unto you. Peace I leave with you, my peace I give unto you: not as the world giveth, give I unto you. Let not your heart be troubled, neither let it be afraid. Ye have heard how I said unto you, I go away, and come again unto you. If ye loved me, ye would rejoice, because I said, I go unto the Father: for my Father is greater than I. And now I have told you before it come to pass, that, when it is come to pass, ye might believe. Hereafter I will not talk much with you: for the prince of this world cometh, and hath nothing in me. But that the world may know that I love the Father; and as the Father gave me commandment, even so I do. Arise, let us go hence.

"I am the true vine, and my Father is the husbandman.       | 133

Every branch in me that beareth not fruit he taketh away: and every branch that beareth fruit, he purgeth it, that it may bring forth more fruit. Now ye are clean through the word which I have spoken unto you. Abide in me, and I in you. As the branch cannot bear fruit of itself, except it abide in the vine; no more can ye, except ye abide in me. I am the vine, ye are the branches: He that abideth in me, and I in him, the same bringeth forth much fruit: for without me ye can do nothing. If a man abide not in me, he is cast forth as a branch, and is withered; and men gather them, and cast them into the fire, and they are burned. If ye abide in me, and my words abide in you, ye shall ask what ye will, and it shall be done unto you. Herein is my Father glorified, that ye bear much fruit; so shall ye be my disciples. As the Father hath loved me, so have I loved you: continue ye in my love. If ye keep my commandments, ye shall abide in my love; even as I have kept my Father's commandments, and abide in his love. These things have I spoken unto you, that my joy might remain in you, and that your joy might be full. This is my commandment, That ye love one another, as I have loved you. Greater love hath no man than this, that a man lay down his life for his friends. Ye are my friends, if ye do whatsoever I command you. Henceforth I call you not servants; for the servant knoweth not what his lord doeth: but I have called you friends; for all things that I have heard of my Father I have made known unto you. Ye have not chosen me, but I have chosen you, and ordained you, that ye should go and bring forth fruit, and that your fruit should remain: that whatsoever ye shall ask of the Father in my name, he may give it you. These things I command you, that ye love one another. If the world hate you, ye know that it hated me before it hated you. If ye were of the world, the world would love his own: but because ye are not of the world, but I have chosen you out of the world, therefore the world hateth you. Remember the word that I said unto you, The

134 |

servant is not greater than his lord. If they have persecuted me, they will also persecute you; if they have kept
my saying, they will keep yours also. But all these things
will they do unto you for my name's sake, because they
know not him that sent me. If I had not come and
spoken unto them, they had not had sin: but now they
have no cloak for their sin. He that hateth me hateth my
Father also. If I had not done among them the works
which none other man did, they had not had sin: but now
have they both seen and hated both me and my Father.
But this cometh to pass, that the word might be fulfilled
that is written in their law, They hated me without a
cause. But when the Comforter is come, whom I will
send unto you from the Father, even the Spirit of truth,
which proceedeth from the Father, he shall testify of
me: and he also shall bear witness, because ye have been
with me from the beginning.

"These things have I spoken unto you, that ye should
not be offended. They shall put you out of the synagogues: yea, the time cometh, that whosoever killeth
you will think that he doeth God service. And these
things will they do unto you, because they have not
known the Father, nor me. But these things have I told
you, that when the time shall come, ye may remember
that I told you of them. And these things I said not unto
you at the beginning, because I was with you. But now
I go my way to him that sent me; and none of you asketh
me, Whither goest thou? But because I have said these
things unto you, sorrow hath filled your heart. Nevertheless I tell you the truth; It is expedient for you that
I go away: for if I go not away, the Comforter will not
come unto you; but if I depart, I will send him unto you.
And when he is come, he will reprove the world of sin,
and of righteousness, and of judgment: of sin, because
they believe not on me; of righteousness, because I go
to my Father, and ye see me no more; of judgment, because the prince of this world is judged.

"I have yet many things to say unto you, but ye cannot

bear them now. Howbeit when he, the Spirit of truth, is come, he will guide you into all truth: for he shall not speak of himself; but whatsoever he shall hear, that shall he speak: and he will shew it unto you. All things that the Father hath are mine: therefore said I, that he shall take of mine, and shall shew it unto you. A little while, and ye shall not see me: and again, a little while, and ye shall see me, because I go to the Father."

Then some of his disciples among themselves said, "What is this that he saith unto us, A little while, and ye shall not see me: and again, a little while, and ye shall see me: and, Because I go to the Father?" They said therefore, "What is this that he saith, A little while? we cannot tell what he saith."

Now Jesus knew that they wanted to ask him, and said unto them, "Do ye inquire among yourselves of that I said, A little while, and ye shall not see me: and again, a little while, and ye shall see me? Verily, verily, I say unto you, That ye shall weep and lament, but the world shall rejoice: and ye shall be sorrowful, but your sorrow shall be turned into joy. A woman when she is in travail hath sorrow, because her hour is come: but as soon as she is delivered of the child, she remembereth no more the anguish, for joy that a man is born into the world. And ye now therefore have sorrow: but I will see you again, and your heart shall rejoice, and your joy no man taketh from you. And in that day ye shall ask me nothing. Verily, verily, I say unto you, Whatsoever ye shall ask the Father in my name, he will give it you. Hitherto have ye asked nothing in my name: ask, and ye shall receive, that your joy may be full.

"These things have I spoken unto you in proverbs: but the time cometh, when I shall no more speak unto you in proverbs, but I shall shew you plainly of the Father. At that day ye shall ask in my name: and I say not unto you, that I will pray the Father for you: for the Father himself loveth you, because ye have loved me, and have believed that I came out from God. I came forth from the Father, and am come into the world: again, I leave the world, and go to the Father."

His disciples said to him, "Lo, now speakest thou plainly, and speakest no proverb. Now are we sure that thou knowest all things, and needest not that any man should ask thee: by this we believe that thou camest forth from God." Jesus answered them, "Do ye not believe? Behold, the hour cometh, yea, is now come, that ye shall be scattered, every man to his own, and shall leave me alone: and yet I am not alone because the Father is with me. These things I have spoken unto you, that in me ye might have peace. In the world ye shall have tribulation; but be of good cheer; I have overcome the world."

Jesus spoke these words, and lifted up his eyes to heaven, and said, "Father, the hour is come; glorify thy Son, that thy Son also may glorify thee: as thou hast given him power over all flesh, that he should give eternal life to as many as thou hast given him. And this is life eternal, that they might know thee the only true God, and Jesus Christ whom thou hast sent. I have glorified thee on the earth: I have finished the work which thou gavest me to do. And now, O Father, glorify thou me with thine own self with the glory which I had with thee before the world was. I have manifested thy name unto the men which thou gavest me out of the world: thine they were, and thou gavest them me; and they have kept thy word. Now they have known that all things whatsoever thou hast given me are of thee. For I have given unto them the words which thou gavest me; and they have received them, and have known surely that I come out from thee, and they have believed that thou didst send me. I pray for them: I pray not for the world, but for them which thou hast given me; for they are thine. And all mine are thine, and thine are mine; and I am glorified in them. And now I am no more in the world, but these are in the world, and I come to thee. Holy Father, keep through thine own name those whom thou hast given me, that they may be one, as we are. While I was with them in the world, I kept them in thy name: those that thou gavest me I have kept, and none of them is lost, but the son of perdition; that the scripture might be fulfilled. And now come I to thee; and these things I speak in the world, that they might have my joy fulfilled in themselves. I have given them thy word; and the world hath hated them, because they are not of the world, even as I am not of the world. I pray not that thou shouldest take them out of the world, but that thou shouldest keep them from the evil. They are not of the world, even as I am not of the world.

"Sanctify them through thy truth: thy word is truth. As thou hast sent me into the world, even so have I also sent them into the world. And for their sakes I sanctify myself, that they also might be sanctified through the truth. Neither pray I for these alone, but for them also which shall believe on me through their word; that they all may be one; as thou, Father, art in me, and I in thee, that they also may be one in us: that the world may believe that thou hast sent me. And the glory which thou gavest me I have given them; that they may be one, even as we are one: I in them, and thou in me, that they may be made perfect in one; and that the world may know that thou hast sent me, and hast loved them, as thou hast loved me. Father, I will that they also, whom thou hast given me, be with me where I am; that they may behold my glory, which thou hast given me: for thou lovedst me before the foundation of the world. O righteous Father, the world hath not known thee: but I have known thee, and these have known that thou hast sent me. And I have declared unto them thy name, and will declare it: that the love wherewith thou hast loved me may be in them, and I in them."

# ✚ *Friday*

When they got to a place called Gethsemane, *Christ in*
he said to his disciples, "Sit ye here, while I go and pray *Gethsemane*
yonder." He took with him Peter, James and John. He
began to be horrified and very depressed and he said to
them, "My soul is exceeding sorrowful, even unto death:
tarry ye here, and watch with me."

He went a short distance further, knelt on the ground
and prayed, "Father, if thou be willing, remove this cup
from me: nevertheless not my will, but thine, be done."
An angel from heaven appeared before him, giving him
strength. Being in agony, he prayed more urgently and
he began to sweat drops of blood which fell down to the
ground.

When he rose from prayer and had come back to his
disciples, he found them asleep because they were worn
out from grief. He said to them, "Why sleep ye? Rise
and pray, lest ye enter into temptation."

While he was speaking, Judas came, who was *The Betrayal*
one of the twelve. With him was a large crowd, armed *and Arrest*
with swords and sticks, which had been sent by the
chief priests and elders of the country. The traitor had
given them a sign which he would use. He had said to
them, "Whomsoever I shall kiss, that same is he: hold
him fast." He came to Jesus at once and said to him,
"Hail, master," and he kissed him. Jesus said to him,
"Friend, wherefore are thou come?" Then they took
hold of Jesus and held him.

Simon Peter, one of those who was with Jesus, reached
and drew his sword. He struck a servant of the high
priest and cut off his ear. The servant's name was Malchus.
Jesus said to Peter, "Put up again thy sword into his
place: for all they that take the sword shall perish with
the sword. Thinkest thou that I cannot now pray to
my Father, and he shall presently give me more than | 139

twelve legions of angels? But how then shall the scriptures be fulfilled, that thus it must be?" At the same time, Jesus said to the multitudes, "Are ye come out as against a thief with swords and staves for to take me? I sat daily with you teaching in the temple, and ye laid no hold on me. But all this was done, that the scriptures of the prophets might be fulfilled."

The soldiers, with their captain and the Jewish police, arrested Jesus, bound him, and took him first to Annas, because he was the father-in-law of Caiaphas, who was high priest that year. It was Caiaphas who had advised the Jews that it would be to their interest for some man to die on behalf of all the people.

Simon Peter and another disciple followed Jesus. That other disciple was known by the high priest and he went with Jesus into the palace; but Peter stood outside the door. Later this other disciple came back and spoke to the woman who kept the door, and brought Peter inside. Then the woman doorkeeper said to Peter, "Art not thou also one of this man's disciples?" He replied, "I am not." The servants and police standing outside had made a charcoal fire, for it was cold. They stood around warming themselves, and Peter stood with them and warmed himself.

*The Trial by the Jews*      The high priest questioned Jesus about his disciples and his teachings. Jesus answered him, "I spake openly to the world; I ever taught in the synagogue, and in the temple, whither the Jews always resort; and in secret have I said nothing. Why asketh thou me? Ask them which heard me, what I have said unto them: behold, they know what I said." After Jesus had said this, one of the police who was standing with them slapped Jesus and said, "Answerest thou the high priest so?" Jesus answered him, "If I have spoken evil, bear witness of the evil: but if well, why smitest thou me?"

So Annas sent him, handcuffed, to Caiaphas, the high priest.

They led Jesus to the high priest, and with him were assembled all the chief priests and the elders and the scribes. Peter followed, from some distance back, on into the palace of the high priest. He sat with the servants and warmed himself at the fireside.

The chief priest and those assembled with him looked for evidence against Jesus which would warrant the death sentence, but they found none. Many gave false witness but their evidence contradicted itself. Some stood and lied against him, saying, "We heard him say, I will destroy this temple that is made with hands, and within three days I will build another made without hands." But on this statement the witnesses did not agree. The high priest stood before them and asked Jesus, "Answerest thou nothing? what is it which these witness against thee?" But he made no reply. Again the high priest asked him, "Art thou the Christ, the Son of the Blessed?" Jesus said, "I am: and ye shall see the Son of man sitting on the right hand of power, and coming in the clouds of heaven."

Then the high priest tore his robe and said, "What need we any further witnesses? Ye have heard the blasphemy: what think ye?" They all agreed that he was guilty and should be put to death.

The men who were holding Jesus began to laugh at him and even spit on him. Then they blindfolded him, struck him on the face and said "Prophesy, who it is that smote thee?" And they spoke vulgar words against him.

As Peter was waiting downstairs, one of the maids of the high priest came in. When she saw Peter warming himself by the fire, she looked at him and said, "And thou also wast with Jesus of Nazareth." But he denied it, "I know not neither understand what thou sayest." He went out on the porch and at that moment he heard the cock crow. The maid saw him again and began to tell those who were standing around, "This is one of them." Peter denied it again. A little later, those standing around said to Peter, "Surely thou are one of them: for thou art a Galilean, and thy speech agreeth thereto." He began to curse, and with an oath said, "I know not this man of whom ye speak." The cock crew a second time. The Lord turned and looked at Peter. Then Peter remembered what Jesus had said to him, "Before the cock crow twice, thou shalt deny me thrice." As he thought about that, he wept bitterly.

As soon as it was daylight, the elders, chief priests and scribes assembled together and had Jesus brought before them. They said to him, "Art thou the Christ? Tell us." He said to them, "If I tell you, ye will not believe: and if I also ask you, ye will not answer me nor let me go. Hereafter shall the Son of man sit on the right hand of the power of God." Then they all said, "Art thou then the Son of God?" He said to them, "Ye say that I am."

They said, "What need we any further witness? for we ourselves have heard of his own mouth."

When Judas, who had betrayed him, saw that Jesus had been condemned to death, he was filled with remorse. He brought the thirty pieces of silver to the chief priests and elders and said to them, "I have sinned in that I have betrayed the innocent blood." They replied, "What is that to us? see thou to that." He threw down the pieces of silver on the floor of the temple, walked out, and went and hanged himself. The chief priests picked up the silver pieces and said, "It is not lawful for to put them into the treasury, because it is the price of blood." They discussed the matter and bought land to be used as a potter's field, as a burial place for strangers. From then on this place was called "the field of blood." In this way the words of the Prophet Jeremiah were fulfilled: "And they took thirty pieces of silver, the price of him that was valued, whom they of the children of Israel did value; and gave them for the potter's field, as the Lord appointed me."

# The Week
## Christ Died

They led Jesus from Caiaphas to the court room, but the Jews stayed outside to keep from being defiled so they could eat the Passover meal. Pilate went outside to them and said, "What accusation bring ye against this man?" They answered, "If he were not a malefactor, we would not have delivered him up unto thee." Then said Pilate to them, "Take ye him, and judge him according to your law." Therefore, the Jews said to him, "It is not lawful for us to put any man to death." Thus they were fulfilling Christ's own prophecy as to how he would die.

*Jesus Before Pilate*

Pilate went back into the court room, called Jesus and said to him, "Art thou the King of the Jews?" Jesus answered him, "Sayest thou this thing of thyself, or did others tell it thee of me?" Pilate answered, "Am I a Jew? Thine own nation and the chief priests have delivered thee unto me: what hast thou done?" Jesus answered, "My kingdom is not of this world: if my kingdom were of this world, then would my servants fight, that I should not be delivered to the Jews: but now is my kingdom not from hence." Therefore, Pilate said unto him, "Art thou a king then?" Jesus answered, "Thou sayest that I am a king. To this end was I born, and for this cause came I into the world, that I should bear witness unto the truth. Every one that is of the truth heareth my voice." Pilate asked, "What is truth?"

Then Pilate said to the chief priests and to the people, "I find no fault in this man." The people grew angrier and said, "He stirreth up the people, teaching throughout all Jewry, beginning from Galilee to this place." When Pilate heard them mention Galilee, he asked if the man were a Galilean. On learning that the man was a Galilean and belonged in Herod's jurisdiction, he sent him to Herod, who was in Jerusalem at that time.

Herod was glad to see Jesus. He had been anxious to see him for a long time, because of many things he had heard about him. He hoped to see Jesus perform some miracle. He questioned him at length, but Jesus made no

| 143

reply. The chief priests and scribes vigorously pressed their case against him. Herod and his soldiers ridiculed Jesus, dressed him in a gorgeous robe, and sent him back to Pilate.

That same day Pilate and Herod became friends, having had a feud between them.

When Pilate had called together the chief priests, the rulers, and the people, he said to them, "Ye have brought this man unto me, as one that perverteth the people: and, behold, I, having examined him before you, have found no fault in this man touching those things whereof ye accuse him: no, nor yet Herod: for I sent you to him; and, lo, nothing worthy of death is done unto him. I will therefore chastise him, and release him."

At that feast, it was the custom of the governor to release to the people a prisoner whom they chose. There was a notorious prisoner, named Barabbas, who had caused insurrection and had committed murder in so doing. When they were gathered together, Pilate said to them, "Whom will ye that I release unto you? Barabbas, or Jesus which is called Christ?" Pilate realized they had brought Jesus before him because they were envious of him.

When he had taken a seat on the court bench, his wife sent word to him, "Have thou nothing to do with that just man: for I have suffered many things this day in a dream because of him." But the chief priests and elders persuaded the people that they should ask for the release of Barabbas, and destroy Jesus. The governor said to them, "Whether of the twain will ye that I release unto you?" They said, "Barabbas." Pilate said to them, "What shall I do then with Jesus which is called Christ?" They all said to him, "Let him be crucified." The governor said to them, "Why, what evil hath he done?" But they shouted louder, "Let him be crucified!"

When Pilate saw that he could gain nothing and a riot was beginning, he took water and washed his hands before the crowd and said, "I am innocent of the blood of this just person: see ye to it." The people answered, "His blood be on us, and on our children!" Then he released Barabbas to them. When he had whipped Jesus, he surrendered him to be crucified.

Then the soldiers of the governor took Jesus into the governor's headquarters and collected the entire guard around him. They undressed him and put on him a scarlet robe. Then they platted a crown of thorns and put it on his head, and a reed in his right hand. They knelt before him and jeered at him, saying, "Hail, King of the Jews!" They spit on him, took the reed and hit him on the head.

Pilate came out and said to them, "Behold, I bring him forth to you, that ye may know that I find no fault in him." Then Jesus came out, wearing the crown and thorns and scarlet robe. Pilate said, "Behold the man!" When the chief priests and the Jewish officials saw him, they shouted, "Crucify him, crucify him!" Pilate said to them, "Take ye him, and crucify him: for I find no fault in him." The Jews answered, "We have a law, and by our law he ought to die, because he made himself the Son of God."

When Pilate heard what they said, he was even more afraid. He went back inside the court room and said to Jesus, "Whence art thou?" But Jesus did not answer. Then Pilate said to him, "Speakest thou not unto me? knowest thou not that I have power to crucify thee, and have power to release thee?" Jesus answered, "Thou couldest have no power at all against me, except it were given thee from above: therefore he that delivered me unto thee hath the greater sin."

From then on Pilate tried hard to release him, but the Jews kept shouting, "If thou let this man go, thou art not Caesar's friend: whosoever maketh himself a king speaketh against Caesar." When Pilate heard that, he brought Jesus forth and sat down in the judge's seat in a place known as "the Pavement" (Gabbatha in the Hebrew language).

It was about noon on the eve of the Passover. He said to the Jews, "Behold your King!" But they cried out, "Away with him, away with him, crucify him." Pilate said to them, "Shall I crucify your King?" The chief priests answered, "We have no king but Caesar." Then he turned Jesus over to them to be crucified. When they had mocked him, they took the robe from him, put his own clothes on him and led him out to crucify him.

*The Cruci-*
*fixion*

As they led him away, they took hold of Simon, a Cyrenian, who was coming in from out in the country, and put the cross on his shoulder and made him carry it along behind Jesus. A large crowd followed, including women who cried and mourned over him. Turning to them, Jesus said, "Daughters of Jerusalem, weep not for me, but weep for yourselves, and for your children. For, behold, the days are coming, in the which they shall say, Blessed are the barren, and the wombs that never bare, and the paps which never gave suck. Then shall they begin to say to the mountains, Fall on us; and to the hills, Cover us. For if they do these things in a green tree, what shall be done in the dry?"

There were two others, criminals, who were with him to be put to death. They marched to a place called "the place of a skull," which in Hebrew is called Golgotha. They offered him a drink of wine mixed with a bitter drug, but when he had tasted it, he refused to drink it. Then they crucified him, and the criminals with him, one on his right and the other on his left. Jesus said, "Father, forgive them; for they know not what they do."

Pilate wrote an inscription and it was put on the cross. It said, JESUS OF NAZARETH THE KING OF THE JEWS. This inscription was read by many Jews, for the place where Jesus was crucified was near the city, and it was written in Hebrew and Greek and Latin. The chief priests of the Jews said to Pilate, "Write not, The King of the Jews; but that he said, I am King of the Jews." Pilate answered, "What I have written I have written."

When the soldiers had crucified Jesus, they divided his clothes into four parts and each of them took a part, excepting his cloak. The cloak was seamless, having been woven in one piece. They said to themselves, "Let us not rend it, but cast lots for it, whose it shall be." Thus the Scripture was fulfilled which said,

> "They parted my raiment among them,
> And for my vesture they did cast lots."

This was what the soldiers did.

Those who passed by shouted abuse at him. They wagged their heads and said, "Thou that destroyest the temple, and buildest it in three days, save thyself. If thou be the Son of God, come down from the cross." In the same manner the chief priests mocked him, along with the scribes and elders, saying, "He saved others; himself he cannot save. If he be the King of Israel, let him now come down from the cross, and we will believe him. He trusted in God; let him deliver him now, if he will have him: for he said, I am the Son of God.

One of the criminals, who was hanging there with him, heaped scorn on him, saying, "If thou be Christ, save thyself and us." The other criminal rebuked him and answered, "Dost not thou fear God, seeing thou art in the same condemnation? And we indeed justly; for we receive the due reward of our deeds: but this man hath done nothing amiss." And he said, "Lord, remember me when thou comest into thy kingdom." Jesus said to him, "Verily I say unto thee, To day shalt thou be with me in paradise.'

Standing near the cross of Jesus was his mother, and her sister Mary, the wife of Cleophas, and Mary Magdalene. When Jesus saw his mother and the disciple whom he loved standing near to her, he said to her, "Woman, behold thy son!" Then he said to the disciple, "Behold thy mother!" From then on that disciple took her to live in his home.

From noon until three o'clock in the afternoon there was darkness over all the land. About three o'clock Jesus cried out loudly, "Eli, Eli, lama sabachthani?" which means, "My God, my God, why hast thou forsaken me?" When some of those standing there heard that, they said, "This man calleth for Elias."

After this, he knew that everything had been accomplished to fulfill the Scripture. He said, "I thirst." Immediately one of them ran and got a sponge, filled it with wine, put it on a stick and put it to his lips. The others said, "Let be, let us see whether Elias will come to save him." When Jesus had received the wine, he said, "It is finished." Then in a loud voice he said, "Father, into thy hands I commend my spirit." Having said that, he died. At that very moment, the curtain of the temple was torn in two from top to bottom. The earth shook and the rocks were split open. Graves were opened and many bodies of the saints came to life and, coming out of their graves after his resurrection, they went into Jerusalem and were seen by many.

Because it was the day of preparation for the Passover, and because bodies should not remain on the cross on the Sabbath, for the Sabbath was a holy day, the Jews requested Pilate to have the men's legs broken and their bodies taken away. The soldiers came and broke the legs of the two who were crucified with Jesus. When they got to Jesus and saw that he was already dead, they did not break his legs. One of the soldiers thrust a spear in his side, and immediately blood and water came out. An eyewitness who could be trusted told that this happened. He knew that he spoke the truth and others would believe, also. These things were done that the Scripture be fulfilled, "A bone of him shall not be broken," and another Scripture which says, "They shall look on him whom they pierced."

That evening, because it was the day before the Sabbath, a man by the name of Joseph, a rich man from Arimathea, a respected member of the Council and

*The Burial*

148 |

one who looked forward to the coming of the kingdom,
openly went to Pilate and asked for the body of Jesus.
Pilate was surprised that he was already dead. He called a
centurion and asked how long he had been dead. When
the centurion told him, he gave the body to Joseph.

Also Nicodemus, who had come to Jesus one night,
came and brought a mixture of about a hundred-pound
weight of myrrh and aloes.

They took the body of Jesus, wrapped it in linen cloth,
folding in the spices, as the Jews customarily bury. They
laid him in Joseph's new sepulchre in which no one had
been buried, and which was cut out of a rock. They
rolled a large stone over the entrance. Mary Magdalene
and Mary the mother of Jesus saw where he was put.
They went back home, prepared spices and ointments
and then rested the Sabbath day, according to the commandment.

## ✠ *Saturday*

The next morning the chief priests and Phari-     *The Sepulchre*
sees came in a group to Pilate and said, "Sir, we remem-     *Sealed*
ber that that deceiver said, while he was yet alive, After
three days I will rise again. Command therefore that the
sepulchre be made sure until the third day, lest his disciples come by night, and steal him away, and say unto
the people, He is risen from the dead: so the last error
shall be worse than the first." Pilate said to them, "Ye have
a watch: go your way, make it as sure as ye can." So they
went, secured the sepulchre by sealing the stone and set
a watch.

# THE
# FORTY DAYS

✝ *From the Resurrection to the Ascension*

*The Resurrec-*
*tion*

When the Sabbath was over, Mary Magdalene, Mary the mother of James, and Salome had sweet spices which they had bought that they might go to Jesus' tomb and anoint his body. At this very time, there came a severe earthquake; an angel of the Lord descended from heaven, came to the tomb and rolled back the stone from the door, and sat down upon it. His face shone like lightning and his clothes were white as snow. The guards about the tomb shook with terror and fell into a dead faint.

At sunrise on the first day of the week, the women went to the sepulchre. As they went, they said to each other, "Who shall roll us away the stone from the door of the sepulchre?" When they arrived they saw that the stone, which was very large, had already been rolled away.

They went into the sepulchre and there saw a young man sitting on the right side, clothed in a long white robe. They were frightened. He said to them, "Be not affrighted: Ye seek Jesus of Nazareth, which was crucified: he is risen; he is not here: behold the place where they laid him. But go your way, tell his disciples and

Peter that he goeth before you into Galilee: there shall ye see him, as he said unto you."

They hurried outside and ran from the sepulchre, trembling in amazement. Because of their fear they said nothing to anyone.

Mary Magdalene hurried to Simon Peter and the other disciple whom Jesus loved, and said to them, "They have taken away the Lord out of the sepulchre, and we do not know where they have laid him!"

Peter and that other disciple went out and ran together toward the sepulchre. The other disciple outran Peter and got there first. Stooping down so he could look in, he saw the linen burial clothes lying there, but he did not go inside. Simon Peter arrived, following him, and went into the sepulchre. He saw the linen clothes lying there, and the cloth which was about Jesus' head was not with the other clothes, but folded together in a place by itself. Then the other disciple who had arrived first at the sepulchre went in also, and he saw and believed. As yet they did not understand the Scriptures which said that he must rise from the dead.

The disciples went back home; but Mary remained outside the tomb, weeping. As she wept, she stooped down and looked into the sepulchre. She saw two angels clothed in white sitting there, one at the head and the other at the feet, where the body of Jesus had lain. They said to her, "Woman, why weepest thou?" She replied, "Because they have taken away my Lord, and I know not where they have laid him."

When she had said this, she turned around and saw Jesus standing there, but she did not know it was Jesus. Jesus said to her, "Woman, why weepest thou? whom seekest thou?" She, supposing him to be the gardener, said to him, "Sir, if thou have borne him hence, tell me where thou hast laid him, and I will take him away." Jesus said to her, "Mary!" She turned to him and said, "Rabboni!" which means "Master." Jesus said to her,

151

"Touch me not; for I am not yet ascended to my Father: but go to my brethren, and say unto them, I ascend unto my Father, and your Father; and to my God, and your God."

Mary Magdalene went and told the disciples that she had seen the Lord and what he had said to her.

As the women were going their way, some of the guards at the tomb went into the city and told the chief priests all that had happened. When they had met with the elders and conferred together, the chief priests gave the soldiers a large sum of money and told them to say, "His disciples came by night, and stole him away while we slept. And if this come to the governor's ears, we will persuade him, and secure you." So they took the money and did as they were told. This story was told all around and is still being told among the Jews even until now.

*The Walk to Emmaus*       That same day two of those who knew Jesus were making their way to the village of Emmaus, which was about seven miles from Jerusalem. They talked to each other about all that had happened. As they talked, Jesus himself came up and walked with them, but they were prevented from recognizing him.

He said to them, "What manner of communications are these that ye have one to another, as ye walk, and are sad?" And the one of them, whose name was Cleopas, answered, "Art thou only a stranger in Jerusalem, and hast not known the things which are come to pass there in these days?" He said to them, "What things?" They replied, "Concerning Jesus of Nazareth, which was a prophet mighty in deed and word before God and all the people: and how the chief priests and our rulers delivered him to be condemned to death, and have crucified him. But we trusted that it had been he which should have redeemed Israel: and beside all this, today is the third day since these things were done. Yea, and certain women also of our company made us astonished, which were early at the sepulchre; and when they found not his body, they came, saying, that they had also seen a vision of angels, which said that he was alive. And certain of them which were with us went to the sepulchre, and found it even so as the women had said: but him they saw not."

Then he said to them, "O fools, and slow of heart to believe all that the prophets have spoken: ought not Christ to have suffered these things, and to enter into his glory?" Then he began with Moses and all the prophets and explained to them all the Scriptures concerning himself.

They came near to the village where they were going. He acted as though he were going on farther, but they insisted, "Abide with us: for it is toward evening, and the day is far spent." So he went in to tarry with them.

As they sat at the table together, he picked up the bread and asked the blessing. Then he broke the bread and gave it to them. Then their eyes were opened and they recognized him; and he vanished from their sight. They said to each other, "Did not our heart burn within us, while he talked with us by the way, and while he opened to us the scriptures?"

They got up during that very hour and returned to Jerusalem. They found the eleven and those who were with them, and said to them, "The Lord is risen indeed, and hath appeared to Simon!" They told what had happened on the road and how they recognized him when he broke the bread.

On the evening of that same day, it being the first day of the week, the disciples were assembled together, with the doors shut because of their fear of the Jews. Jesus came and stood among them and said, "Peace be unto you." When he had said this, he showed to them his hands and side. The disciples were filled with gladness when they saw the Lord. Then Jesus said to them again, "Peace be unto you: as my Father hath sent me, even so send I you." When he had said this, he breathed on them and said, "Receive ye the Holy Ghost: whose so-

*Christ's Appearance to the Disciples*

| 153

ever sins ye remit, they are remitted unto them; and whose soever sins ye retain, they are retained." Then he asked them, "Have ye any meat?" They gave him a piece of broiled fish and some honeycomb. He took it and ate it before them.

One of the twelve, Thomas (called the twin), was not with them when Jesus came. The other disciples told him, "We have seen the Lord!" He replied to them, "Except I shall see in his hand the print of the nails, and put my finger into the print of the nails, and thrust my hand into his side, I will not believe."

*The Confession of Thomas*

The following week the disciples were again together in the room and Thomas was with them. Even though the doors were shut, Jesus came and stood among them and said, "Peace be unto you." Then he said to Thomas, "Reach hither thy finger, and behold my hands; and reach hither thy hand, and thrust it into my side: and be not faithless, but believing." Thomas answered. "My Lord and my God!" Jesus said to him, "Thomas because thou hast seen me, thou hast believed: blessed are they that have not seen, and yet have believed."

*The Great Draught of Fishes*

Afterward Jesus again showed himself to the disciples at the sea of Tiberias. It was this way: together were Simon Peter, Thomas, Nathanael of Cana in Galilee; the sons of Zebedee and two other disciples. Simon Peter said to them, "I go a fishing." They said to him, "We also go with thee." They immediately went and got into a ship. But they caught nothing that night.

When morning came, Jesus stood on the shore, but the disciples did not know it was Jesus. Jesus said to them, "Children, have ye any meat?" They answered, "No." He said to them, "Cast the net on the right side of the ship, and ye shall find." They cast as he told them and caught so many fish they were not able to pull them in. Then that disciple whom Jesus loved said to Peter, "It is the Lord!"

When Simon Peter heard that it was the Lord, he threw

is fisher's coat around himself (for he was naked), and plunged into the sea. The other disciples came in a small boat, pulling the net with the fish; for they were not far from land, only about a hundred yards.

As soon as they got to the shore, they saw coals of fire with fish laid on them, and some bread. Jesus said to them, "Bring of the fish which ye have now caught." Simon Peter went and pulled in the net which was filled with a hundred and fifty-three large fish. Yet in spite of the fact there were so many, the net was not torn. Jesus said to them, "Come and dine." None of the disciples dared ask him, "Who art thou," for they knew it was the Lord. Jesus came up, took the bread and gave it to them, and likewise he gave them the fish. This was the third time that Jesus showed himself to his disciples after his resurrection from the dead.

When they had eaten, Jesus said to Simon Peter, "Simon, son of Jonas, lovest thou me more than these?" He said to him, "Yea, Lord; thou knowest that I love thee." He said to him, "Feed my lambs."

He said to him a second time, "Simon, son of Jonas, lovest thou me?" He replied, "Yea, Lord; thou knowest that I love thee." He said to him, "Feed my sheep."

He said to him a third time, "Simon, son of Jonas, lovest thou me?" Peter was bothered because he said to him the third time, "Lovest thou me?" and he said to him, "Lord, thou knowest all things; thou knowest that I love thee." Jesus said to him, "Feed my sheep. Verily, verily, I say unto thee, When thou wast young, thou girdedst thyself, and walkest whither thou wouldest: but when thou shalt be old, thou shalt stretch forth thy hands, and another shall gird thee, and carry thee whither thou wouldest not." He said this to reveal the manner of death by which Peter was to glorify God. When he said this, he then said to him, "Follow me."

Peter turned and saw the disciple whom Jesus loved following. This was the one who had leaned close to Jesus

at the supper and asked, "Lord, which is he that betrayet
thee?" Seeing him, Peter said to Jesus, "Lord, and wh.
shall this man do?" Jesus said to him, "If I will that h
tarry till I come, what is that to thee? Follow thou me
Then it was told around within the brotherhood that th
particular disciple would not die; yet Jesus did not sa
that he would not die, he only said, "If I will that he tarr
till I come, what is that to thee?"

It was this same disciple which told of this and wrot
it, and we know that his testimony is true.

*The Great
Commission*

Then the eleven disciples went into Galil
to a mountain where Jesus had arranged to meet then
When they saw him, they knelt before him, though som
of them doubted. He said to them, "All power is give
unto me in heaven and in earth. Go ye therefore, an
teach all nations, baptizing them in the name of th
Father, and of the Son, and of the Holy Ghost: teachin
them to observe all things whatsoever I have commande
you: and, lo, I am with you alway, even unto the end c
the world. Amen." And he said to them, "Go ye int
all the world, and preach the gospel to every creatur
He that believeth and is baptized shall be saved; but h
that believeth not shall be damned. And these signs sha
follow them that believe; In my name shall they cast ou
devils; they shall speak with new tongues; they shall tak
up serpents; and if they drink any deadly thing, it sha
not hurt them; they shall lay hands on the sick, and the
shall recover."

*The Ascension*

He said to them, "These are the words whic
I spake unto you, while I was yet with you, that all thing
must be fulfilled, which were written in the law of Mose
and in the prophets, and in the psalms, concerning me.
Then he opened their minds so they might understan
the Scriptures, and said to them, "Thus it is written, an
thus it behoved Christ to suffer, and to rise from the dea
the third day: and that repentance and remission of sin
should be preached in his name among all nations, begin

156 |

ing at Jerusalem. And ye are witnesses of these things.
And, behold, I send the promise of my Father upon you:
but tarry ye in the city of Jerusalem, until ye be endued
with power from on high."

Then he led them out as far as Bethany. He lifted up
his hands and blessed them. As he was blessing them, he
was separated from them and carried up into heaven and
sat on the right hand of God. They worshiped him and
returned to Jerusalem with great joy, and they spent their
time in the temple, praising and blessing God. And from
there they went and preached everywhere, the Lord
working with them and confirming their words with
miracles that followed.

Jesus did many other things in the presence of *Many Other*
his disciples which are not recorded in this book; but *Things*
these things have been written in order that you might
believe that Jesus is the Christ, the Son of God, and that
in the act of believing you might possess **eternal life**
through his name.